No One Cheers for Goliath

My Leadership Story

By Timothy J. Brown, Ph.D.

Edited by Laura H. Brown, Ph.D.

Foreword by Angelina Pettinati

On the Cover:
Baby Picture
Assistant Coach with the Falco Falcons
Childhood home in South Coatesville, PA
The former Lukens Steel Plant
Presentation at West Chester University
High School Graduation Picture

Cover Photo Arrangement by Joe Cornelius

Interested in having Dr. Brown for a speaking engagement?
Contact him at: tjbrown712@gmail.com

ISBN: 978-0-578-75551-9

Monday Creek Publishing
Ohio USA

"With God all things are possible."
- Matthew 19:26 (NIV)

Table of Contents

Acknowledgments

One of my first childhood memories is of waking up early in the morning and following my brother and sister downstairs to eat breakfast before they left for school. Although I didn't have to wake up early, as I was not old enough to go to school, I wanted to be like my older brother and sister. I looked up to them, I wanted to be like them, and I wanted to be with them. To their credit, I don't recall them minding me "getting in the way" as we had one small bathroom everyone had to use in order to get ready for school. As soon as they got up, I got up. I rushed to use the bathroom, got dressed, and ran down the stairs to make it to the dining room table. Before I hit the top of the stairs, I could smell breakfast. The smell of bacon filled the house, as my mom flipped and stacked pancakes for my brother and sister. And there I was rushing down the stairs to be with them.

I give a lot of credit to my mom as she was the one who kept everyone organized. My dad would be the first one down; she would get him ready, then my siblings. What I appreciated was my mom never told me to go back to bed or that I was disrupting her as she got my brother and sister ready for school. When I got downstairs, I would get a plate, knife, and fork, and sit down at the table—ready to eat. When I sat at the table, she would simply look me in the eye and ask in a friendly tone, "How many pancakes would you like?" That was a leadership moment right there—my mom adapted to me being at the table, and she made me feel welcomed. I was with my siblings even though I wasn't going to school with them. But she let me be part of it—even down to having my hair combed. Then, when it was time for them to go, I would follow them to the door and watch as they walked down the street to school. I remember this daily routine, and they never got tired of me.

It has been said many times that "everybody has a story to tell" with my story being no exception. It takes encouragement, though, and support to go from having a story to actually putting it down on paper and having the courage to share your story with others. The impetus for writing my story emerged from motivational speeches I presented using examples from my lived experience to support ideas and principles. As I continued to speak and write on other subjects and heard the stories of others, I began to seriously consider putting my own ideas down on paper.

Then, the opportunity came. When I announced in December 2016, I would not seek a fourth term as Chair of the Department of Communication Studies at West Chester University (I was in the role since 2007), this gave me the opportunity to look back on my improbable journey. It was a journey I began as a first-generation college student from Coatesville, PA and all the events in between to my eventual election as department chair. I oversaw a program of 500 plus majors and over 35 faculty members at the same institution from which I had graduated. I knew I had the material to convey my story. I felt it was a story that would inspire and motivate others. The idea was further cemented in January of 2018 when I was invited as a guest speaker and participant for Macmillan Publishers Retreat in Boston. I had met Allen Cooper, Program Manager for Macmillan, the previous fall at our National Communication Association conference during a workshop on student learning outcomes for the communication discipline. I was able to share my story with Allen at dinner the night before the retreat and he intensely listened. His encouragement was the last push I needed to "write my story."

This book would not be possible without my wife, Dr. Laura Hamilton Brown. She has been a bedrock in my academic journey, and she has made me a better person, husband, father, and leader. She hasn't let me settle for "good enough," and she always pushed me to maximize my skills and abilities even when I had self-doubt.

We met as graduate students at Ohio University in the School of Interpersonal Communication (which is now the School of Communication Studies in the Scripps College of Communication). I am forever grateful for her intellect, and her writing and editing skills that elevated my writing into a strength as opposed to a weakness. This book is another product of her love and support.

In addition, this book would not be possible without my two sons, Jordan Josef Brown and Isaiah Hamilton Brown. You are my joy and my delight. Both of you are growing up into fine young men. I appreciate that no matter how many times I tell the stories from my childhood, some included in this book, you always humor me by listening and responding. Thank you for your encouragement.

Finally, I would like to thank my extended family, friends, mentors, colleagues, and students who have made this book possible. There are too many to name, but I truly appreciate all of your contributions to this endeavor.

Foreword

Most of us have no idea at the start what we're meant to do, or even what we're capable of. Some of us don't even find our 'thing' so much as it finds us. And sometimes, it's only because of some special person who introduces us to possibilities we might never have imagined for ourselves.
- Leslie Odom Jr.

Dr. Tim Brown can look at you as if he's seeing the person you will become 20 years from now. He's challenged me to think bigger and to work harder; he allowed me to assist in his classes, and he hired me for my first teaching job, but most importantly he's always believed in me. He saw my failures as great experiences; he saw my accomplishments as Olympic victories, and he saw my potential when I believed there was none. When I walked into his office over 10 years ago, I had no idea I was about to meet the man who would change the course of my future.

As an undergraduate, I knew him as Dr. Brown. Later, when I became a colleague, I would know him as Tim. On that day many years ago, however, I was waiting for him in his outer-office on the fifth floor of Main Hall at West Chester University. I had just transferred from Temple University and had taken summer classes in order to be accepted into the Communication Studies major. As I waited, my anxiety grew. I wasn't sure how a department chair would relate to me. I saw so many awards and plaques on his office walls, and wait—was that a picture of him with Brian Dawkins? I was a bit intimidated. To my surprise, when he walked in, he greeted me with a smile, a quick chat about the Philadelphia Eagles, and then he proceeded to look at my transcript. My GPA had come up short by .002 to be accepted into the major. This was my failing point. I had already switched schools and transferred majors. I was unsure where my academic career was headed. However, Tim simply looked at me, smiled and said, "Welcome to communication studies."

A great leader has vision. They can see and plan for a victory 10 years from now. Upon completing my undergraduate degree, Tim told me I could go on to grad school. I had never had anyone say that to me before. I felt as though I barely graduated on time, was lucky to have landed an internship and now here I was being told I could go on to grad school. That's the thing about Tim. Once you get comfortable, he'll challenge that space and have you reach for something greater. When I was completing the program and considering graduate school, Tim told me he was teaching a summer course and asked if I would like to be his course assistant. He explained it would be great practice for graduate school. I loved teaching with Tim. He was constructive, insightful, and inspiring. "Consistency is key" he would say. "What you say and what you do for one student must be consistent with what you would do for others. It is a way to measure fairness, and a way for students to have clear expectations of what you will and will not budge on."

Tim completes his work with a team mindset. He's always thinking about who can help with a certain task. He trusts people to help him but also gives them the chance to learn. When you are hungry for, have a desire for success and a thirst to prove yourself but you have no idea where to start, you need someone like Tim to give you a chance. Over the years, I observed that giving people a chance was a primary characteristic of his leadership style. I was one of many individuals who benefited from his leadership.

While living and working in Pennsylvania and applying to grad schools, I was denied by most and "conditionally" accepted by the University of Northern Colorado. Tim said, "Get all A's your first semester in order to declare your program and when you graduate, it's most likely you can be hired to teach." That's exactly what happened. I moved across the country even though everyone in my family had lived within a five block radius in Delaware County for generations. I went because Tim told me I could. Tim sets people up for success without micromanaging. He'll assign a task and then trusts people as their work unfolds. In my own example, he was confident in the path I chose, and he was excited that I would accomplish a goal differently than he would. Overall, he provides the blank canvas and the brushes but allows the person to paint. He provides the tools and the assignments but lets the person create. His approach to managing people is best illustrated by what Steven Spielberg said, "The delicate balance of mentoring someone is not creating them in your own image, but giving them the opportunity to create themselves."

When I returned from Colorado, I began teaching at West Chester University for the next four years. During those four years, Tim taught me many things. The first thing he said when I came on board as an adjunct was "Don't get too comfortable." He explained, I shouldn't get too comfortable as an adjunct because I might not push forward to complete my Ph.D. He also cautioned, "You're young and you're a female—students will want to test you. Start the semester strong and firm; you can always relax as the semester goes on. However, you will have a hard time gaining respect if you start lenient then try to be more firm as an instructor."

The first time we worked on a paper together and submitted it to the Eastern Communication Association conference, it was denied. When I emailed Tim to tell him the news he said, "No worries—it's all part of the research process. Even the lion is only successful 1 out of 20 times." When I didn't get into a Ph.D. program right away, he said, "Let's get you ready for fall." Whenever I tried to self-sabotage my own talents, voice, research interests, he would keep me grounded. "No, you should still write about this, find the gaps, find out what is missing, find out what people are not saying and go there." He never lost touch, enthusiasm or faith.

My own experience working with Tim is just one example of his servant leadership style which he discusses in detail in his book *No One Cheers for Goliath*. *No One Cheers for Goliath* chronicles Tim's stories in leadership—his personal reflections on the people and events that shaped his leadership philosophy, which is forged on building authentic relationships and providing individuals with opportunities and support in order for them to succeed. He believes in people because others believed in him. He supports people as others supported him. He connects with people as others have connected with him. His ability to see people through their challenges is reflective of the challenges he had to overcome. The people, events, and circumstances that Tim discusses in *No One Cheers for Goliath* are meant to motivate, to encourage, and to inspire leaders and aspiring leaders. As a result, effective leadership is a transformative process where the leader comes alongside others to unlock their potential in order for them to reach goals that might otherwise have seemed unobtainable.

- *Angelina Pettinati*

Preface

There may never be another Wilt Chamberlain. NBA.com characterized Chamberlain as "basketball's unstoppable force, the most awesome offensive force the game has ever seen."[1]

Basketball historian Leonard Koppett stated that Chamberlain was "the most dominating player who ever played basketball."[2] Despite having left the sport over 40 years ago, Chamberlain's mastery of the game of basketball can be illustrated by his mind-boggling accomplishments that still impact the game today. Chamberlain still holds several NBA records such as: the single-game scoring record (100), the highest single-season scoring average (50.4), the single-season scoring record (4,029), the single game rebounding record (55), the highest single-season rebounding average (27.2), the single season rebounding record (2,149) and the highest single-season minutes average (48.5). During his career, Chamberlain was a 13-time NBA All-Star, 11 time NBA rebounding champion, 7 time

NBA scoring champion, 4 time NBA Most Valuable Player, and 2 time NBA Champion. His number 13 was retired by three NBA teams (Warriors, 76ers, and Lakers) and his collegiate team, the University of Kansas. What might be more astonishing is he *never* fouled out in 1,205 regular-season and playoff games. Overall, Chamberlain holds 72 NBA records, 68 of which he holds by himself.[3]

Chamberlain's career and legacy might best be explained by Hall of Famer and NBA legend Kareem Abdul-Jabbar who stated, "Wilt was one of the greatest ever, and we will never see another one like him."[4]

Chamberlain's records, while outstanding on their own, are even more incredible given several rule changes that were made in an effort to reduce his dominance on the court. For example, the width of the NBA's foul line was widened from 12 to 16 feet to make it more difficult for Chamberlain to score in the low post. Furthermore, offensive interference became a rule to reduce Chamberlain's ability to slam home dunks. Another rule change to limit Chamberlain's dominance was eliminating the practice of lobbing the ball from the baseline directly over the backboard (to Chamberlain). All of these rule changes remain today.

There were big men before Chamberlain but none possessed the combination of offensive and defensive prowess like Wilt. To see Chamberlain play was to see a grown man make other grown men look like boys. While enabling him to excel on the basketball court, Chamberlain's physical and athletic superiority, along with his intellect, created unrealistic expectations from fans. Fans expected him to always do well, to always dominate, to always win. For Chamberlain every record, every win, every score, block, or rebound over time became expected and underappreciated—his superhuman performances were shrugged off as just another day at the office.

Few athletes ever experienced the burden carried by Chamberlain. It was a burden best articulated by Chamberlain himself when he said, "Nobody roots for Goliath."[5] This statement is weighty on many different levels. Chamberlain succinctly articulated America's fickleness with great athletes—the public often loves the underdog and hates the talented rival. As a result, the superior athlete becomes "Goliath," the person to root against rather than for. That's America.

Chamberlain's comment applies not only to athletes but also to leadership. No matter how competent, experienced, and driven you are as a leader—your work and effort often will be overlooked, underappreciated, and taken for granted. No one cheers for Goliath because Goliath is *supposed* to win. The public hates Goliath's talents, skills, and abilities.

Just as no one cheers for Goliath, no one cheers for the leader. The weight of leadership is the same burden that Chamberlain carried. As a leader, expect to be criticized, to be rooted against, and to be undermined no matter how effective you are. Much like Chamberlain, being a leader means being in the midst of a battle between those who are committed to teamwork and sacrifice to achieve organizational goals and those who resist the leader and are driven by self-centeredness, paranoia, and dysfunction.

No One Cheers for Goliath conveys my leadership story from the various leadership positions I have held—most notably the 10 years (2007-2017) I served as Chair of the Department of Communication Studies at West Chester University of Pennsylvania. This book was written to highlight the leadership lessons learned in order to encourage and motivate leaders and aspiring leaders. Being a leader is about keeping one's sanity in a sea of foolishness, maintaining character and composure despite the drama while holding firm to your values and principles to assist, inspire, and motivate others. *No One Cheers for Goliath* is an auto-ethnography offering stories, anecdotes, examples, and principles that provide clarity and perspective for leaders and aspiring leaders to make sense of the nonsense that all leaders will confront.

Chapter 1: It's Not Nature or Nurture, It's Attitude

It was a moment that has always stayed with me. There I was, a first-generation college student sitting in the office of the department chair. Normally, you would think sitting in the office of the chair meant there was a problem or issue or complaint as department chairs often deal with and resolve many problems including student issues. However, mine was different. The department chair was different. The interaction was different. At the time, I knew him as Dr. Klinzing, the long-time chair of the Department of Communication Studies at West Chester University. Unlike other authority figures with whom I had come into contact with, Dr. Klinzing was relational. He would ask you questions, he would ask follow-ups, and if you gave him a lame answer, he'd say, "Come on, Tim, that is a bunch of crap!" Dr. Klinzing or "Denny" as I called him, after I became a faculty member in the same department in which I was once an undergraduate student, was a person who connected with people. He was a leader of people, not a leader of things.

When you are young, life can be a maze—you are moving in contradictory directions, hitting roadblocks, and learning how to navigate the world as you move around, under, and over walls.

Years later as a grown man, I look back at that moment in the fall of 1990 in Denny's office and realize how he saw *me*—he saw me as human, as valuable, as intelligent, as worthy of a discussion as opposed to a lecture. He didn't hide behind policies or proce-dures. He saw people as enactors of policy. For the first time in 20 years, I was coming out of my shell as a guarded, first-generation, young black man from Coatesville, PA, trying to find his way in a foreign environment. West Chester University might have been only 20 miles from my hometown, but it was truly another world. I didn't have conversations or interactions with adults other than my parents. If I did have interactions with others who did not look like me, they were often impersonal and condescending because they didn't see me. They saw my blackness and all the stereotypical ways in which people, especially white people, related to black people. Black people know exactly what I'm talking about. My ex-perience with white people, especially white people in authority, was one of indifference toward me—as if black youth didn't have intelligence, feelings, thoughts, ideas, desires, or dreams. Add that I was a tall, lanky young black man, and I was very self-conscious and shy. I was a turtle who kept his emotions inside his shell. I couldn't show vulnerability; I had to be tough. I had to be mindful of my actions and how I carried myself.

But that moment in time, in Denny's office, was definitely different. He saw me as a person. He saw me as a student with intelligence, with drive, with goals, with dreams. It was one of the first moments in my life where I was developing my own humanity, learning it was OK to speak up, to express myself (in the company of white people), to set goals, and, more importantly, to be relational and to be helpful. I was in Denny's office because I had just completed my internship at FOX 29 Philadelphia in their sports department, and Denny had just finished reading my internship paper. He contacted me to stop by his office so he could congratulate me on the work I did. "Holy Cow, Tim, you did a nice job!" I remember Denny saying, "You should think about graduate school. You have the ability to be a good graduate student." When Denny said that, I almost went into shock. "Graduate school?" I said, "Nah, I want to get a job." Unflinchingly, Denny said, "Anybody can get a job! My old man got a job. The university exists to change students' lives. That's what I believe and that's what I do. And I know you are the type of person who can go on to get his degree and to do the same for others."

At this point, I have to backtrack because up until this point in my academic career there were very few indicators, and I mean very few indicators, suggesting I was graduate student material. In fact, after my first semester at West Chester University I landed on academic probation. It took a lot of work to raise my overall GPA to a 3.0 by senior year. Previous to WCU, I was an average student who graduated from Coatesville Area High School. For the most part, I found the high school curriculum uninteresting and uninspiring. By luck I stumbled upon a TV class (after switching out of a typing class) during my junior year. Reporting the school news each morning on the school's closed-circuit TV system along with the weekly show that was broadcast locally on cable TV was enough to make my last two years of high school enjoyable. Overall, I liked school because I could play sports and while I wouldn't say I was in the popular crowd, I was an amiable person who got along with almost everyone.

It was the student banter and the endless zany moments of high school that kept my interest. Something funny was always happening that kept us laughing. I didn't have to apply myself much, but I did experience a lot of entertaining moments. I remember many comical events which occurred in 11th grade chemistry class. Whenever there was an experiment, someone would always break something or burn something to the amusement of the class. I remember one day one of my classmates talked back to the teacher saying, "Get off my back!" Our teacher who was an older man and close to retirement shot back, "That's right, I'm on your back! I'm on your back!"

In 12th grade, I was in an advanced physics class. I was one of the worst students in the class. The teacher would post the class rankings of students from 1 to 30 based upon their class grade average. I was always one of the bottom three. Anyone who took physics could see the rankings posted at the back of the classroom. It's one thing to know you are struggling in class; it's another for everyone else to actually see it on paper. Anyone who took physics could see the rankings posted at the back of the classroom. After a while, my friend and I would list the current top 20 college football teams next to the top 20 students. The teacher was not amused, but we figured we might as well have fun with the list. It was comical each week when the student list was updated. We wanted to see, "Who's Oklahoma?" "Who's Alabama?" "Who's Penn State?" Seeing who was in the top 10 each week was almost as exciting as who was in the actual NCAA top 10 each week.

There were so many moments that were funny in that class! We would always begin class with equations to solve. The teacher would give us a problem, and he would provide certain numbers. We had the opportunity to use our calculators to get the correct answer. The first one to get the correct answer would get extra credit points. Needless to say, I never received any extra credit points because I did not know what I was doing. I remember the teacher saying to the class how easy it was because all the equations were posted around the room. He would say, "It's easy people; all the answers are around you." I remember thinking, "Yeah, but that only works if you know which equation to pick!"

Another source of comedy in that class was the teams we worked in. Each week there were different stations around the room and each team would work at a station, determine the answer, then move on to the next station. The ironic occurrence in my case was the bottom ranked students were always in the same group. You can't reach high when no one in the group knows how to reach. We were literally, the "blind leading the blind."

One time our group had to lead the experiment at one of the stations. It was the ball drop station. Our team (of bottom ranked students) had to make the calculations for a ball drop experiment. The ball drop experiment involved dropping a small metal ball down a ramp and off a table to land on a calculated place on the floor. Once the calculations were made, the group would put a piece of paper, that had a bull's eye on it, on the ground to predict where the ball would land. When a team led an experiment, everyone in the entire class watched in order to understand how the experiment worked. So naturally when I learned our group was going to lead the ball drop experiment, I knew it would not go well. But, sometimes you have to "put on a good face" and be your own cheerleader. We tried to "fake it until you make it." We worked together, we did our best with the calculations, and we talked ourselves up that we could do it. We did such a good job of pumping ourselves up that I started to actually think we *could* do it.

Our time came. The teacher asked if we were ready. I said we were. All the students gathered around our table. My job was to drop the ball down the ramp. My teammate placed the piece of paper with the bull's eye on the floor. I confidently placed the ball at the top of the ramp. I heard the ball roll off the ramp, roll off the table, then hit the ground. There was a moment of silence. At that moment, I thought we at least hit the paper. I asked my teacher, "Did we hit it?" He responded, "Not even close." Then, the entire class went crazy with laughter. Oh well.

Despite the distractions, I was able to navigate my high school days due to the influence of my mom and dad. I was the third of four kids who would graduate from the Coatesville Area School District. My parents made the necessary interventions, calls, and meetings with teachers and principals over the years to ensure I was getting an education which meant keeping me out of the lower tracked classes. Interestingly, I saw a recent report ranking Pennsylvania 47th (out of 50 states) in the opportunity gap between black and white students—meaning black students as compared to their white peers have less access to small classes, certified teachers, and advanced coursework.[6] As I reflect upon my schooling, I was fortunate to have involved parents.

Both my mother and father were instrumental in my upbringing. When I think of my mother, she was the most positive person I ever met. She grew up in what we would consider today as a poor family in Downingtown, PA. My maternal grandmother was largely a single parent raising a total of seven children. My mother was the oldest girl in her family which meant she assumed many household responsibilities, and she did a lot of the mothering her siblings needed. When we would get together as an extended family, there would always be laughter whether it involved current events in our lives or past events when they would reminisce about growing up on Bradford Avenue in Downingtown. Looking back, I can see that my mom was always the mom. She was a mom to her siblings, then to her own kids, to my cousins, to the neighborhood kids, and later on to her grandkids. She was the mother figure. When we were growing up there were numerous times when someone else was at our table or someone else at our house. She enjoyed people, she saw the good in people, and she made our home a welcoming environment for family and friends.

In the midst of all our activities—school, sports, friends, games, dinners—I never remember my mother being rushed, out of sorts, irritated, or not being willing to help. She always made people feel welcomed, and she always had something positive to say. My mother had a great sense of humor; she enjoyed laughing, and many times when we had company, they would laugh together. Laughter was a great escape and a way to cope with life. Although, as a black woman, my mother dealt with numerous negative incidents, and she missed out on many opportunities women today take for granted, she was never bitter about her circumstances or life choices. She didn't let circumstances steal her joy. She was the glue that held our family and extended family together.

I remember when I was about three or four, I would get excited and immediately run to the window when I heard the garbage truck coming up the street. There was something about the garbage man riding on the back of the truck and pulling the lever to compact the trash that I found fascinating. As a preschooler when people asked me what I wanted to be when I grew up, I would say with excitement, "A trash man!" My mother, in her uncanny ability to see the good in everything, would say, "In some places, trash men make good money." It was a subtle act but an important one to me. I knew in my mother's eyes, my ideas mattered, I mattered. It was important to me because I was a very sensitive boy growing up. As a child, I was a homebody, and I didn't like change. I was content being at home and being my mother's shadow—I needed that extra security to build me up during my upbringing.

My dad, meanwhile, was the strong and quiet type. He grew up in Coatesville, PA the oldest of four siblings. He graduated from the Coatesville Area School District and worked for 40 years at

Lukens Steel Company in Coatesville. He also served his country when he was drafted by the U.S. Army and served overseas in Germany (1961-1963) during the Cold War in the 27th Field Artillery Unit, the Third Armor Division. I was always amazed at the artillery photos from my dad's picture album. It was always interesting learning about his experiences from boot camp to sailing across the ocean to being stationed in Germany. Through it all, my dad was the embodiment of integrity, commitment, and consistency. In his 40 years as a steel worker, he never missed one day of work. No matter how he felt, he went to work. I remember when we bought a fish tank and the metal flip top cut him on the knee when he was putting it together. It was a pretty big gash. The next morning, however, there was my dad with a pronounced limp walking down the street to go to work.

My dad had mouths to feed, so he worked. In those days, Lukens Steel had several shifts, and it was not uncommon for my dad to work double shifts—leaving early in the morning and sometimes not coming back until late at night. Lukens Steel was well-known for making steel plates—part of the steel structure that remained standing at ground zero in New York City after the 911 attacks was made with steel from Lukens.[7] Looking back, although the work was hard, dangerous, and monotonous, I never heard my father complain or vent about his work—he was a provider and that was what he did. We were a working class family, but we always had enough to eat, a roof over our heads, and clothes on our backs. We were also one of the few black families (at least among my friends) who had an intact household with both parents. To my parents' credit (they were married for 54 years), they made a commitment to stay together, to raise us, and to give us opportunities they could only dream of.

So imagine that moment in Denny's office. I was a kid who was moving through life content with the status quo—simply trying to "get a job." No one other than my parents had taken an interest in me. I figured if I "do what I needed to do," I'd be OK. But it changed that day in Denny's office. Denny gave me a vision; he gave me something to aspire to. He not only saw me as a capable person but as a person with worth. Over time, he introduced me to his contacts and his network. He was vouching for me. Through Denny, I would come to know several influential professors such as Dr. Diane Casagrande, Dr. Michael Pearson, Dr. Kevin Dean, Dr. Carolyn Keefe, and Dr. Jim Trotman. These individuals would shape me in my transformation as a person and as a leader.

I learned a lot from all these relationships and from my work with these individuals. I learned that effective leaders must build effective relationships. An effective leader uplifts, inspires, and motivates through leadership. An effective leader assists them in reaching their goals, gives them the opportunity to succeed, keeps track of their achievements, and then celebrates those achievements with them. Leaders have to be genuine and they have to be involved. More importantly, leaders have to have a keen eye to recognize the potential in others and to assist them in their development to succeed. Such leaders have a vision or global perspective that is promoted among the individuals he or she supervises. The effective leader assists individuals in finding their role within that vision or global perspective. Effective leaders take risks and are willing to fail. When there is failure, the effective leader owns up to it, explains what happened and learns from it. They can overcome failure because their body of work proves without a doubt they are working on behalf of the vision or global perspective. Michael Jordan summed it up best when he stated: "I've missed more than 9000 shots in my career. I've lost almost 300 games. Twenty-six times, I've been trusted to take the game winning shot and missed. I've failed over and over and over again in my life. And that is why I succeed."[8]

When I was a department chair, for the most part, I saw very few examples of effective leaders. The leaders who I reported to or who were in higher leadership positions lacked interpersonal skills, did not have emotional intelligence, did not care about individuals, did not know how to reach out or relate to others who were not like them, passed the buck, gave people the run-around, were not genuine, hid behind policies and procedures, and spoke eloquently of ideas such as diversity while consistently acting in ways that devalued diversity. These leaders did not build effective relationships, but I did observe and experience the cliques these leaders created. What is needed are leaders who know how to build teams not cliques. Creating cliques insulates those in leadership not only from other perspectives and ideas but from a diverse population whom the leader is supposed to represent.

Creating cliques not only separates the leader from different perspectives but is a sign of atrophy. Effective leaders should be growing and developing just like any other person in the organization. Insulating oneself from others is like a person working out only one set of muscles—while one area might be strengthened, the rest of the body will be underdeveloped. As a result, the whole body suffers and is not working towards its potential. When the organization hires or promotes only the same individuals, it is limiting its potential while its diverse population is neither valued nor efficiently utilized.

Effective leadership is an attitude! The attitude of the leader is what drives the culture of an organization. What makes an effective leader is not necessarily nature versus nurture. Instead, effective leaders know how to build genuine and authentic relationships. How many leaders have the skills to build genuine and authentic relationships? How many leaders have the ability and insight to see the potential in individuals? How many leaders have the compassion and the courage to reach out to individuals who are not like them? Few leaders do this. However, at that moment in Denny's office, he was reaching beyond himself. He was building a relationship with me. He was expanding his global perspective by including me in it. And through many interactions that followed over the years, he taught me many leadership skills that would equip me for a lifetime. By unlocking my potential, it impacted my destiny, and my destiny impacted the destiny of others. That is effective leadership. That is the attitude of a true leader.

Chapter 2: Lead People, Manage Things

January 1992: AT&T released the video phone ($1,499); the Americans with Disabilities Act became law; serial killer, Jeffrey Dahmer, pleaded guilty but insane; and #2 Washington defeated #4 Michigan in the Rose Bowl 34-14. The Rose Bowl might not be as weighty as the other events, but as a former Michigan fan, some things never change . . . the Wolverines lost the Rose Bowl, again! January 1992 also marked the month I began graduate work for my M.A. in Communication Studies at West Chester University.

After graduating from West Chester University with a B.A. in Communication Studies in the spring of 1991, I took a newspaper sports reporter job at the now defunct *Coatesville Record*. I was working for my local hometown paper covering high school sports —primarily my former high school, the Coatesville Area Senior High School Red Raiders, and its rival, the Downingtown High School Whippets.[9] I enjoyed going to the games, taking notes, interviewing coaches and players, then heading back to the newspaper office to write my story. It was fun in the beginning, no books, no home-work — just watch games, and write about them. I enjoyed seeing the development of the team I was covering. I had the opportunity to get to know the team, its coach, and players and how their season was unfolding.

I was also able to cover some sports I was less familiar with, but in time I became very knowledgeable and even enjoyed covering them. One sport I had never followed was field hockey. When I went to my first field hockey game, I was clueless. But as the season progressed, I learned the game, and I actually looked forward to covering field hockey; it had lots of action. I remember covering the Downingtown High School field hockey team and their run through the District 1 playoffs; it was exciting! One day when I arrived at the office, the sports editor left me a note: "Carol Haiko (Jill Haiko's mom) called to thank you for your excellent coverage of field hockey. She says you are very fair, polite and write a very honest, sincere article."

The note was a pleasant surprise. I kept it as one of my mementos from my sports reporter days.[10] It also provided me with a key lesson in leadership—to acknowledge and commend the hard work and contributions people make. But also to be genuine and authentic. To be acknowledged, especially for a sport I initially did not follow, motivated me more when I wrote my articles. The note also symbolized how much I had developed as a writer. As I mentioned, I wasn't the best or the most prepared student. English, especially writing, was my worst subject. To this today, I am still the world's worst speller. When my kids are in the mood to tease me, they say, "Dad, how do you spell . . ." Then, we would bust out laughing. But I would get in the last word by saying, "Yeah, but I got three degrees!"

As a freshman at West Chester University, I had to take remedial English. In the basic writing class, I soon realized how poor my writing skills were. In fact after the first semester, I failed ENG 020 and earned a D in Spanish 101 which put me on academic probation. I would have to retake ENG 020 and pass with a C- or better in order to move on to the English composition courses. Coming home with a 1.9 GPA after the fall 1987 semester was one of the worst feelings in the world. I had some doubt whether I would be able to make it.

My difficulty with basic writing gave me flashbacks to 10th grade English. One of the weekly assignments was to spell and define 20 vocabulary words. Since I was the world's worst speller, it was a torturous class! I struggled greatly in that class. My mother should have received the lifetime Mother Theresa award as she patiently worked with me each week on those 20 words. Compounding my struggle, I was not well-read, so I didn't have a wide vocabulary. The vocabulary words were long words, unusual words people did not use in daily conversation—at least not in the conversations I had or heard. I had to remember how to say, spell, and define the words, many of which had the same prefix. The day I received the list, I would come home and write down all the words along with their definitions. My mother would quiz me, over, and over, and over during the week until I had the information well-memorized. It took all my faculties to keep the list, the spellings, and the definitions straight. I'm amazed I made it through 10th grade English.

To make matters worse, Shakespeare was also part of the class. I remember we had to memorize a section from one of Shakespeare's works. Looking back, why we had to do this, I don't know, but I'm damn sure I didn't learn anything from it. I could barely read Shakespeare let alone memorize and repeat the section to the class. Tenth grade English was agony—it's astounding that I was able to improve my writing so quickly when I reached West Chester University.

But I did. Being a former high school athlete, my competitive instincts drove me. When I returned for the spring semester of 1988, I wanted to do better. I was determined to do better. I remember the second professor I had for basic writing was kind and more motivational in her approach to teaching basic writing. Today, we would identify her approach to teaching as being "student-centered." She made the student experience the center of her teaching, and she used her expertise as a teacher to reach the student. She invited us to incorporate our interests and experiences into our writing. She encouraged us to seek her help, if we were having problems, and she made herself available to discuss writing ideas before an assignment was due. I remember she suggested we purchase a grammar book so we could learn how to edit our own papers. She also encouraged us to write about what we were interested in. I didn't know it at the time, but these student-centered principles—encouraging students to seek assistance, being available and accessible, wanting students to succeed, empowering students to take ownership of their work, and incorporating student interests into the learning process would become central to my approach as a faculty member and a driving component when I was department chair. I would build a career as an effective, student-centered teacher and engaged scholar. In fact, in 2019, I was honored by the Eastern Communication Association as a Distinguished Teaching Fellow and a Distinguished Research Fellow—awards very few faculty qualify for or receive. I was humbled by this honor and from the letters of support from former students which reaffirmed my approach to teaching (I have included two of these letters in Chapter 8). My student-centered approach was a philosophy influenced by the teachers from whom I learned the best. Interestingly, reflecting back on my time in that basic English class, I was learning not only how to be an effective writer but how to be a successful leader. Equipping others to be successful and taking the time to support them, assists the leader in building relationships. In the process, it enables the leader to lead people as opposed to managing things.

What I appreciated about her approach to teaching was she met me at my level. She didn't dwell upon my deficiencies or see me as a lost cause. She identified my weaknesses and deficiencies, and one-by-one, she gave me strategies and the knowledge to become a competent writer. What I had to do was take a big step and trust her. After all, she was nothing like me. She was an older grandmotherly figure—probably in her 60s, with white hair, and glasses. However, I had no choice but to trust her; I was on academic probation, I was a poor writer, and I had to pass the class. Once I went to her, and I started to improve, my confidence grew. As I achieved a level of competence, she gave me other skills to work on and master. She had the ability to separate my inability to write from my intelligence. She had the patience and confidence to unlock my intellect, and she did so through her student-centered principles. In the process, I gained hope. As I began to succeed, it led to more confidence, and more confidence led to more success. I would bring my grammar book with me to our meetings and slowly I started to understand the parts of a sentence and the rules of grammar. I started to identify the mistakes I was making, so I could begin to self-edit my work. As I improved my writing, I was able to articulate my ideas more clearly.

I remember the final paper I had to write was a comparison and contrast essay. It was an essay that had to be completed in class during the final exam period. I looked over the assignment and the comparison and contrast could be written either point-by-point or block style. I liked the point-by-point style as I figured I could keep track of the points I was making. For the topic, I immediately thought of a comparison and contrast between Magic Johnson and Larry Bird. Before I started, I approached her at her desk and asked if I could write on the topic. She smiled at me and said, "Great topic, I can't wait to read it." Armed with confidence, I returned to my seat and wrote a four page paper comparing Magic and Bird. Never in a million years would I have imagined comparing two NBA players would be an approved topic for a college-level English paper. However, it enabled me to pass the course. More importantly, I gained valuable writing skills. Things were looking up for me!

Given my struggles with writing, I felt I had a long way to go to become a graduate student. As you can imagine, my hesitation to apply for graduate school was legitimate. As a first generation college student, receiving a B.A. was my Mount Everest. Now, you're asking me to consider a M.A. What if the work is too hard? What if I don't understand the material or can't relate to it? What if I can't write the papers? There was a lot of doubt. It took two phone conversations for Denny to convince me, but by January 1992, I had enough courage to try. The newspaper job while interesting was already losing its luster. My initial enthusiasm for covering high school sports—going to games, interviewing coaches and players and writing up stories quickly became monotonous. The work was not challenging and the pay was terrible. I think I was earning either $10.00 or $20.00 an article—hardly a living wage. So, I tried graduate school and received a graduate stipend as a graduate assistant. It was a change I was ready for.

If you knew Denny, you would know he is a people person and he believes in people. He is also an idea person. If the idea proposed aligned with the program, he would get behind it. Large or small. I remember one time, he asked me to help him clean out a storage room in the basement of Main Hall. Denny's idea was if we cleaned up the place, the space could be used as an extra office or lounge area. I have to mention Denny had a bad back. Even after several surgeries, he continued to struggle with back issues. Eventually, by 2007, his back issues contributed to his retirement as chair and faculty member at WCU. At this moment, however, in 1992 we were working. Denny saw a buffer one of the janitors had left in the room.

"Have you ever used one of these before?" Denny asked.

"No, I haven't," I said.

"It can't be that hard," Denny said. "Why don't you plug 'er in for me?"

As soon as I did, the buffer turned on. All I heard was a loud *"frrrrrmmmm"* as Denny's legs flew out from under him. He twirled for half a turn, holding on for dear life, spun off the buffer and was thrown into a metal framed shelf that came crashing down. There was Denny on the floor—there was a brief silence.

"Are you OK?" I asked.

Denny gets up and starts to laugh, "That wasn't a bright idea! What was I thinking?"

Then, we both started laughing. What I appreciated about that moment was Denny was being human. He didn't carry himself like he was a big shot, a know-it-all, or someone who was too busy for people. He was comfortable around people; he was himself. He was genuine and his words aligned with his actions. Observing Denny showed me true leaders are people who are comfortable with themselves and are comfortable around other people. Denny was committed to people. When he encouraged me to attend graduate school, he also committed to helping me succeed. He was involved in my progress as a student and as a person. He was building a relationship. Although this specific moment did not go well, it was an idea important enough to try. He cared. Many leaders I have observed are the opposite. They don't care, and they don't build genuine relationships.

To his credit, Denny built relationships with everyone, and he extended his own network to include me. My first graduate assistantship was with the WCU Forensics Team (speech and de-bate team) led by Dr. Kevin Dean. Denny showed confidence in me by awarding me the assistantship despite my not being on the team as an undergraduate. However, he believed my knowledge of speech, my demeanor, and my organizational skills would be a good fit for the team. He was right. I enjoyed coaching and assisting the team which succeeded at both the state and national levels. In addition, I learned a great deal about responsibility as I was han-dling the tournament funds for the team (paying tournament fees, hotel accommodations, distributing meal money, etc.), driving the team in the university van to events, supervising the team at the tournament, etc. Other graduate assistantships I had at WCU in-cluded assisting with Dr. Michael Pearson's large-lecture course and being one of the first graduate assistants for the Frederick Douglass Institute (FDI) with Dr. Jim Trotman who was FDI's Founder and Director. In addition, I was an academic tutor and course assistant for the Academic Development Program's (ADP) speech courses during the summer working under the direction of Dr. Kevin Dean. When I was a doctoral student at Ohio University, Denny also hired me in the summers of 1995 and 1996 as an ad-junct to teach a speech class at West Chester University which en-abled me to return home during the summers. In each position, I grew as a person and as a scholar, and learned a great deal about teaching, how to interact with faculty and students, and how to be a leader. All of the individuals to whom Denny introduced me and whom I worked with believed in building relationships and helping others. I spent time with each of these individuals, and they had a profound impact on my development as a person and as a leader. I'm proud to say I am still in contact with them all and value their friendship and mentorship.

When I was chair of the Department of Communication Studies at West Chester University, between 2007-2017, the examples and ideas I learned from all these individuals shaped my current student-centered, servant-leader philosophy. I took pride in my role as a campus leader who served on and led many university committees, yet I didn't miss a beat when it came to running the department. From scheduling, to advising, to hiring, to evaluations and observations, I did it all. And I still maintained an active research agenda. Furthermore, I kept an open door policy when I was in my department office. Individuals were always welcomed. Students were always welcomed. Being in a large institution (and as a product of the institution), I knew first-hand how impersonal it could be. When I became department chair, I wanted to be helpful. It was a principle I learned from my late mother; she would always say, "Be a help, not a hindrance." She lived that principle, and I believed in it as a faculty member and department chair. When I was department chair, not a day passed when I didn't help someone with a question, issue, or problem. I became very efficient at multitasking and problem-solving. If I couldn't directly help a student, I would at least point him or her in the right direction.

Some people thought I was crazy for having an open door policy. But my thought was although an unexpected visitor might extend my day or interrupt my work, this interruption could make a vital difference in the visitor's life. Case in point: One day, a young man contacted our department secretary and said he had an urgent matter which needed my attention. When he arrived, I invited him in. In his rush, he explained very quickly how he was through with the major, and he wanted me to sign off on paperwork to change his degree to Professional Studies.

Me: "Let's back-up. What's the problem? Why do you want to change your major?"

Student: "I'm having trouble with Spanish. I can't pass it. I'm going to need to change my major to Professional Studies which does not require a language."

Me: "Let me look at your degree progress report and see if that is the best decision for you."

After looking at his degree progress report, the student was a few credits shy of graduating with a Communication Studies degree, but he needed to complete SPA 102 with a C- or better. He was closer to completing his degree in Communication Studies than completing a second minor which was required for a Professional Studies degree.

Me: "Look, you are better off staying with Communication Studies. You like the major, right?

Student: "Yes"

Me: "And you want to graduate next semester, right?"

Student: "Yes."

Me: "Alright, all you have to do is pass SPA 102 with a C- or better. You don't have to be the world's best Spanish student; you just need a C-. I wasn't good at Spanish, but I passed it. Ask around for a good instructor, someone who will work with you and will assist in your learning to pass the class."

Needless to say, the student did go on to pass SPA 102 and complete his Communication Studies degree. In fact, he went on to be a graduate student in our master's program, and I had him as a student in one of the courses I taught. He was really sharp as well as a deep thinker. We had several talks about him pursuing a Ph.D., and I told him not to think it was out of reach. I told him my own story and how I thought a Ph.D. was not possible. My story inspired him. He stopped by many times and we talked about the process. When he decided to apply to doctoral programs, I assisted with his applications. Eventually he selected Denver University. Today that young man is a college professor. Back then, when he was accepted into the Denver program, he wrote me a letter thanking me. In his letter he wrote:

Dr. Brown

After hearing of my recent acceptance to the Communication Studies Ph.D. program at Denver University, it would be a travesty if I did not send a letter of my sincere appreciation for what you've done for me at West Chester over the past several years. I began the program as the stereotype of a young college kid in culture shock, lost in a social environment that I had never experienced before. The backlash to the self-centered choices made during my years of undergrad culminated in our meeting whether I should finish as a Communications major, or my idea, which was to register as a professional studies major. This meeting is almost [the] ultimate dirty secret of my life that I will forever be ashamed of because the thought that I even entertained finishing with a professional studies degree due to bad grades and general misguided decision-making is disheartening, embarrassing, and disgraceful. If it was not for you giving me guidance, and recognizing I did in fact have some potential, my entire life would be completely different. If it was just for that half hour you took out of your schedule to move me in the right direction, I am still forever indebted to you. Still, to this day, my family makes fun of me about the day I almost became a professional studies major.

Beyond this obvious gesture, after I began the master's program and took your classes, you pushed me down a new avenue toward a profound appreciation and understanding of cultural communication. I have never really expressed this to you before, but that [graduate] class sincerely changed my perspective on all communication. It allowed me, for the first time, to see the matrix of cultural dominance through words and how it exists in every language and every culture. For this too, I am forever grateful, as it has shaped the way I teach all of the subjects in my classes, and above all else, changed my perception of life and communication outside of academia.

There are several people who played integral roles in my life outside of my immediate family, and I can definitely say that you are one of them. If it wasn't for your constantly taking time to guide me down the right path, I would probably be a washed-up musician struggling to get by with no hope in the future. Instead, because of your genuine selflessness and concern for others, you made me a Ph.D. candidate. Whether it was my indecisiveness about career choices, or uncertainty about academia, or need of a reference, or need of a teaching job, you always had my interests in mind regardless of the number of responsibilities you already had to fulfill. I am sorry for the wordiness and formality of this letter, but I really owe you so much, and I don't know how to repay you for how significantly you've changed my life in a positive direction. The only thing I can offer is to say that if you ever need anything at all, even in the slightest sense, I will always answer the call and have your back. You're one of the greats, as an administrator, teacher, and person and I hope this sappy thank you letter doesn't ruin our friendship! Please keep in touch, and I will make sure I always represent my people at West Chester with hard work, dignity, and honesty, the same way you ran the department.

Much thanks and appreciation

When I think back to that moment with my former student, the student's situation was very similar to my own graduate experience. That advising moment underscores, with all the duties and responsibilities a leader has, people are the most important. Leaders lead people and manage things. Unfortunately, from what I have observed, too many leaders have this the other way around and are bean counters who treat people as if they are things. However, if the leader is attuned to people and knows something about their drive and ambitions, people will go beyond what is necessary in order for the organization to move forward in excellence. In contrast, if a leader treats people as things, tasks will get done, but the leader will get only a person's minimal effort at best.

Leaders, effective leaders in any profession have to build relationships with people in order to lead. The people you work with are people not things. One of the best examples reinforcing the importance of people over things was broadcast in ESPN's *30 for 30* series. The series was initially intended for 30 different filmmakers to create 30 different sports documentaries on various sports topics, events, and individuals. Originally meant for 30 topics, the series has produced over 90 films. One episode in the *30 for 30* series chronicled the Celtics/Lakers rivalry.[11] The three-part documentary traced the histories of the two storied franchises, addressed the racial subtext between the two teams, reviewed their championship history and focused on the rivalry via Magic Johnson and Larry Bird in the 1980s. The documentary took me back to that basic writing course final in which I wrote a comparison and contrast paper on Magic and Bird!

One part of the documentary that influenced my leadership philosophy was when coach Pat Riley had to make a decision concerning the team. Briefly, it was the second straight year that the Celtics/Lakers were meeting in the NBA Finals. In the previous year, the Lakers felt they had the better team but lost extending their championship drought against the Celtics (at that point, the Lakers had never defeated the Celtics in the NBA finals; they were 0-8). In the 1985 finals, the Lakers dropped the first game in the series, and its long-time leader, Kareem Abdul Jabbar, had one of his worst games in recent memory. The press suggested that at 38 years old Kareem was done and the Lakers would once again fall to the Celtics.

The part that was fascinating to me was the segment when the Lakers were taking the team bus from the hotel to the Boston Garden for Game 2. One of Riley's team rules was only players, no spouses, no family members were allowed on the team bus. Upon boarding the bus for their important Game 2 match-up, Kareem asked Lakers Coach, Pat Riley, if his dad could sit beside him on the bus ride to Boston Garden. In the episode, the documentary explained how Riley was a stickler for rules. He also, however, sensed the fragile psyche of his team and of Kareen who was the team's captain. At this point in the documentary, Riley talks about the moment and his thought process at the time. Riley thought to himself, if his captain, a multiple league MVP needed his dad at that moment sitting with him on the bus, Riley was not going to let a rule, he made, disrupt his captain and impede the team's effort to win the critical game.

When the players boarded the bus, and they saw Kareem in the first seat sitting next to his dad, Riley adapted. Once the team was seated on the bus, Riley seized the moment and gave an impromptu speech about the importance of dads. He talked about his own dad and explained what he learned from his dad. One lesson he learned was to stand firm. Riley explained when opposition comes your way, you have to stand up and confront it. Riley told the Lakers they needed to stand up and confront the Celtics—don't back down. In the episode, the players explained how they reflected on the first game and how they didn't stand up to the Celtics. They were motivated by Riley's speech. More importantly, Riley was sensitive enough to recognize Kareem's humanity and related to him as a person. Riley adapted and seized upon the opportunity to motivate not only Kareem but the entire team. Instead of missing the moment, Riley had the emotional intelligence to adapt and motivate his players.

Riley's sensitivity to know what Kareem and his team needed was rewarded as Kareem went on to have his best game of the series as the Lakers won Game 2 *and* eventually the series. The Lakers first championship win against the Celtics would propel the Lakers to win three championships in four years. Their success can be attributed to Riley knowing he was managing people and not things. A leader will always get more out of people when the leader values them and what they bring to the table as opposed to having a rigid system that forces people into prescribed ways of accomplishing tasks.

I love this example because it clearly reaffirms that effective leadership is based on being in relationship with people and managing individuals who are human beings, not robots. I'm convinced that many leaders, if they were Riley during that moment, would have been tripped up by blindly following specific rules or by following unquestioned processes. Effective leaders need emotional intelligence and must have the conviction to make tough decisions regardless of what others might think. After all, the leader has a global perspective that others don't.

Leaders should never forget people are their greatest asset. And the leader must be the one to create a genuine relational environment. The leader must not build up walls, must not be unavailable, and must not be dictatorial. I'm a firm believer: "rules without relationship lead to rebellion." Leaders must be in relationship with the individuals they are leading. When individuals feel they are heard and understood, they can accomplish anything as a team.

Chapter 3: If There Is No Struggle, There Is No Progress

Frederick Augustus Washington Bailey, or as he was better known, Frederick Douglass, was one of the most influential Americans of the 19th Century. Born a slave, Douglass escaped slavery to become a national and international giant in the abolition movement. He was a social reformer, orator, writer, newspaper editor, and statesmen. He was an informal advisor to Abraham Lincoln and he helped recruit African Americans to serve in the Civil War. Douglass wrote three autobiographies. His first one, *Narrative of the Life of Frederick Douglass, An American Slave* (1845), was a best seller that propelled Douglass into national and international prominence. Douglass' introduction in the *Narrative* hauntingly framed the inhumanity of slavery and the racist ideology that fueled it:

I WAS born in Tuckahoe, near Hillsborough, and about twelve miles from Easton, in Talbot county, Maryland. I have no accurate knowledge of my age, never having seen any authentic record containing it. By far the larger part of the slaves know as little of their ages as horses know of theirs, and it is the wish of most masters within my knowledge to keep their slaves thus ignorant. I do not remember to have ever met a slave who could tell of his birthday. They seldom come nearer to it than planting-time, harvest-time, cherry-time, springtime, or fall-time. A want of information concerning my own was a source of unhappiness to me even during childhood. The white children could tell their ages. I could not tell why I ought to be deprived of the same privilege. I was not allowed to make any inquiries of my master concerning it. He deemed all such inquiries on the part of a slave improper and impertinent, and evidence of a restless spirit.[12]

As a graduate student at West Chester University, I had the privilege of working as a graduate assistant for the Frederick Douglass Institute and its Director, Dr. Jim Trotman. There are many adjectives I can use to describe Dr. Trotman: passionate, noble, generous, engaging, thoughtful, dedicated. To me and others, Dr. Trotman was an unwavering pillar of support and a champion of social justice who engaged individuals with a humility and sensitivity that no one could match. To hear Dr. Trotman present was to hear a masterful speaker who would captivate a room with his intellect and wit. He had an inviting presence that commanded attention. He was a strong, black man of character, dignity, and faith. Working under his leadership, I gained a full understanding of how to keep focus, how not to get too low when there were challenges and how not to get too high when there was success. Dr. Trotman was the tour-de-force behind the establishment of a Frederick Douglass Institute on each campus in the Pennsylvania State System of Higher Education. What I appreciated about Dr. Trotman's leadership was his unique ability to share the credit in a genuine way with those around him. And he remembered the most specific details about people. Often during his guest lectures and presentations, he knew how to acknowledge and build up key people who were part of the event or occasion, and he did it with style.

Dr. Trotman's connection to Douglass was further strengthened when it was discovered that Douglass gave his last public speech at West Chester University in 1895.[13] Thus, Jim Trotman's effort to enlighten the campus and the community about Douglass' work and to integrate Douglass' ideals of equality, empowerment and liberty into the curriculum was given new urgency.

When I was a graduate assistant for the Frederick Douglass Institute, Douglass' work influenced my own. In speaking on West India Emancipation in 1857, Douglass was forecasting what he perceived as the inevitable fight for the emancipation of African Americans. Douglass stated:

> Let me give you a word of the philosophy of reform. The whole history of the progress of human liberty shows that all concessions yet made to her august claims have been born of earnest struggle. . . .. If there is no struggle there is no progress. Those who profess to favor freedom and yet deprecate agitation are men who want crops without plowing up the ground; they want rain without thunder and lightning. They want the ocean without the awful roar of its many waters. This struggle may be a moral one, or it may be a physical one, and it may be both moral and physical, but it must be a struggle.[14]

Douglass elegantly and unapologetically reminds us that change is brought about by struggle, and struggle and change are intertwined. You can't have one without the other. Douglass' words are a great reminder for leaders that struggle is inevitable. There will be struggles to implement the vision; there will be struggles to maintain harmony; there will be struggles with individuals who will struggle against you; there will be struggles when you least expect them; and there will be struggles long after you thought issues were resolved.

Douglass also reminds us that life is a struggle. My struggles began even before I was aware of them. In 1969, I was born with a club foot. To straighten my foot, doctors "reset" the alignment of the bones and put my foot in a cast. For several years, I had to wear special shoes to ensure my foot would straighten out. Although I don't remember wearing the special shoes, they did the job as I would later play sports through high school. It was an expensive process, but my parents were able to afford the special shoes I needed. When I was older, my mother told me when I was a baby lying in the crib, I would raise my foot with the special boot and bang it on the crib railings to signal when I was ready to get out.

In 1971, when I was two years old, my parents moved from Downingtown to Coatesville to the neighborhood of South Hill. The move put my dad closer to work—he could walk to work—which allowed my mother to use the car during the day. The neighborhood of South Hill in South Coatesville was a working-class neighborhood. It was situated on a hill in between the city of Coatesville to the north and Lukens Steel Company to the south and west. Also, South Hill was located next to the Oak Street Housing Projects (which no longer exist today). The housing projects consisted mostly of black families while South Hill was where the white people lived. When our family moved to South Hill in 1971, we were the first black family on our street. As my parents would tell the story, the day after we moved into our house on Remington

Avenue, "for sale" signs went up among the other houses on the street. No one wanted to live next to a black family.

Not deterred, my parents raised us four children in that small house that had one bathroom and no air conditioning. As we grew and made friends with the neighborhood kids, most of the neighbors warmed up to us as a family. By the time my older siblings were in middle school, our family had become a pillar in the neighborhood and South Hill was more integrated with many black and brown families. In a short time, my parents went from being outsiders to stalwart members of the South Hill community.

The point to keep in mind for any leader is there are always going to be people, issues, and circumstances working against you. As a leader, you have to be aware there will be struggle. Struggle and leadership go together like peanut butter and jelly, like ice cream and cake, like Sanford and Son. If you don't like struggle, don't take a leadership position. However, if you see conflict, contention, and challenges as opportunities, then leadership is for you. In these situations, with diligence, hard work, and consistency, you can make a positive impact and eventually earn the respect of others. But leaders should always keep in mind, the more you accomplish, the more struggles you will face.

I opened this chapter with Douglass' *Narrative* as he articulated his struggle with not knowing his age. Even after he was a well-known national and international figure, he still grappled with not knowing his birth date. It was a struggle he endured his entire life. This point should remind leaders the struggles we face, even from years past, will impact our leadership. A pivotal moment that forever shaped my leadership approach occurred in 1985 when I played high school football at Coatesville Area Senior High School. Then, as it is now, Coatesville is a staunch supporter of its high school sports teams, especially football and basketball.

As I mentioned, I was a sensitive kid growing up. One of the areas that helped me develop as a person was sports. When I was young, kids in my neighborhood played sports—every day. We played football, basketball, wiffleball, curve ball, etc. Sometimes we played before catching the school bus and sometimes when we got home after practice. If we were not playing sports, we were watching them on TV. What I liked about sports was you were able to compete and you were able to achieve based upon your own abilities. If you played well, you won. If you did not play well, you lost. If you lost, you worked to get better. I wasn't the most athletic kid, but through hard work and practice, I became pretty good. I was one of the neighborhood kids who produced. Sports also gave me my first leadership opportunities. Since I was one of the better players, the other kids looked to me for direction and organization. We organized our own games, made the ground rules, and handled disputes. As a chosen captain, I learned the strengths and weaknesses of the other kids, how their abilities fit on the team, how to coach them, and how to motivate them. Looking back, I realize I learned a lot of invaluable lessons from playing sports and organizing the neighborhood kids. These lessons served me well later on in my leadership positions such as department chair and dean. I didn't recognize it at the time, but the skills I learned organizing the neighborhood kids were the initial foundation for how to lead people.

Since I lived for sports, I was influenced by what I saw on TV It's hard to imagine today, but TV back then was not the 24-hour juggernaut it is now. Growing up, you could see your local team as long as it was not blacked out. In the Philadelphia area, there were only eight to ten channels. There was NBC channel 3, ABC channel 6, and CBS channel 10 and the local channels 17, 29, and 57 along with the local PBS station, channel 12. Sports were not televised as widely then as they are today. I even recall one year the NBA finals being on taped delay—something unthinkable today! I remember one time watching the MLB All-Star Game on TV. At that time, the American and National Leagues didn't play during the season—only at the All-Star game and at the World Series. (Needless to say, I'm not a fan of interleague play, the three divisions, or the wild card.) After watching the game and talking to my friends, we decided to have our own All-Star Game. I took the responsibility of organizing the neighborhood kids. We would separate into the Americans and the Nationals and have our All-Star Game at Green

Field (which was down the street from my house). Everyone brought a t-shirt to the field and we used red or blue crayons to write numbers, names, and stripes on the t-shirts. My friend's mom worked at Jamesway (which was like K-mart), which meant we could purchase red and blue caps at a discount. We organized a date. We worked on the field. We had our little sisters as cheerleaders. People came out to watch. It was an event!

While we as kids and the community members who came out to the game enjoyed the event, not everyone was pleased. Years later my mom told me, she received a call from my friend's mom who was upset her kids had ruined their t-shirts with crayons. My mom took it in stride and listened politely to the other mom complain about the ruined t-shirts. After a while, my mom heard enough and told the other mom, "If the t-shirts mean that much to you, I'll buy you new ones." That ended that conversation.

I enjoyed playing football, basketball, and baseball in that order. After middle school, I played football and basketball. By 11th grade, I was only playing football. Football was my sport. I was rail thin, but I was tough and confident, and I knew the game. At that time, Coatesville ran an option attack and I played the quarterback position well. I didn't have the strongest arm, but I had a lot of natural leadership skills. The kids listened to me, and I knew the plays. I could run the offense as I knew my keys and I would correct players if they were out of position. In 8th grade at South Brandywine middle school, I had some competition—Teon Lee. Teon, even as an 8th grader, looked the part of a football player. He was built; he was athletic; and he must have been 6-foot-tall in 8th grade. Nevertheless, I was confident in my abilities and so was Teon. As QBs, we worked together a lot and eventually became friends.

Interestingly, while Teon had all the physical skills, he was injury prone. I had to stay prepared because it was likely that Teon would get hurt. That year Teon did get hurt. He started the season hurt, came back in the middle of the season, then got hurt again. When I was inserted into the line-up, I didn't miss a beat. We actually moved the ball well when I was the quarterback. In one game, I remember throwing two TD passes against our rival North Brandywine, and I remember beating Gordon (which was a tough team that consisted of kids from the city of Coatesville). We went undefeated our 8th grade year and were the unofficial "City Champs."

Years later, when I was a faculty member at WCU and was serving on jury duty, those memories came back in an unexpected way. Now, serving on a jury is a serious duty, and I remember how quiet it was when the judge led the jury into chambers to start our deliberations. As I walked down the hallway, a delivery man appeared at the other end of the hallway. As I continued down the hallway with the other jurors, and I got closer to him, we both looked at each other. It was Galen Williams whom I had thrown those two TD passes to in the North Brandywine game after all these years. As I started to head into chambers, I heard Galen yell loudly, "Tim Brown, I thought that was you! That's my quarterback! That's my quarterback!" It brought a smile to my face.

In ninth grade we had two football teams. I was the QB for one of the teams. In 10th grade I was the back-up JV QB and defensive safety. But 11th grade was when everything changed. That year, I was the first team JV QB for all practices and in the three scrimmages. But for the first JV game, the coaches put in a sophomore to start. During the week, I went back to the first team for practice, but the same thing happened for the second JV game.

I remember one of the players asking me. "Why aren't you playing?" I said, "I don't know." That night, my dad asked me why I wasn't playing and I told him the same thing, "I don't know." I could tell that my dad was not pleased with the situation. Although he didn't say anything else at dinner, I didn't know my dad was planning to speak to the coach. At the end of the next practice, I was walking off the practice field, and there was my dad next to my QB coach whose face was as red as a stop sign.

My dad: "Tim, your coach needs to talk to you."

QB Coach: "Timmy, I apologize, if we weren't clear. I know that you have done everything that we have asked you to do. And you have improved 100%. But the coaching staff wants to see the younger guy and give him some reps. We think you can be a good receiver because you know the plays."

Next to watching my mother die of pancreatic cancer, this was one of the most devastating moments in my life. A 16-year old's dream of playing QB for the Coatesville Red Raiders was nuked in ten seconds. Suddenly, the reality of race and sports became very apparent to me.

I could no longer be naïve about how the world works. I realized that for better or for worse, my blackness would impact my opportunities or the lack thereof. At that moment, I stopped drinking the red and black Kool Aid of Coatesville Area Senior High School. The reality was life is not a fairy tale where hard work alone is rewarded. Life is especially unfair for black folk, and full of contradictions, indignities, and power relationships that have to be navigated. I was living in a world where I was the outsider and there was nothing that anyone could do about it. And this would not be the last time. It's a struggle that black people have to confront in all areas of life. I had spent a career in the Coatesville system, yet they didn't know me or see me. It's the dilemma of being black in America.

In the '80s, black quarterbacks were uncommon (and even today there continue to be many stereotypes black quarterbacks have to confront, a subject I have written about[15]). My reality was typical for many blacks who played the QB position. I had a difficult time processing being denied the *opportunity* to compete for the position. It's one thing, if I competed and failed, but to not even have the opportunity made it worse. It's a struggle African Americans face in all aspects of life—institutional racism negates African Americans from having opportunities at every life juncture. At that time, Coatesville was not ready for a black quarterback.

Reflecting back on that moment, I'm not sure how I moved past that decision. I did for a short time contemplate quitting, but I was not a quitter. I stayed on the team, but that moment killed my passion to play. I also remember the head coach talking to me. I think he was concerned that I would quit football and play basketball. He kept stressing how I would be able to earn a varsity letter by playing receiver, and how I would make a good receiver. I was further taken aback when he explained I would be the ideal receiver as I knew the plays and wouldn't forget the verbiage when I ran in with the play to give it to the quarterback. Man, he had no idea how insulting that was! In short, he trusted me to take in the play, but he did not want me as the primary person to execute the play.

Years later I was able to process that moment within the complicated history of Coatesville, PA and its intersecting challenges of race, power, and opportunity. Coatesville, 39 miles west of Philadelphia, is midway between Philadelphia and Lancaster, PA. Coatesville's location made it a desired stop on the Philadelphia to Lancaster Turnpike which was one of the first paved roads in the United States dating back to 1795. Today, that road is known as

U.S. Route 30 which runs through the center of town. In Pennsylvania, one could travel Route 30 from Philadelphia in the east to Pittsburgh in the west. Up until 1996, Coatesville had regional rail service to Philadelphia through the Southeastern PA Transportation Authority (SEPTA).

Historically, Coatesville was one of the stops on the underground railroad as the city was roughly 15 miles north of the Mason-Dixon line which separates Pennsylvania from Maryland. With the steel mill located on the west branch of the Brandywine Creek, African Americans who settled in Coatesville could earn a living wage by working in the mill. The steel mill's origins date back to 1793, making it one of the oldest in the country. In 1825, it was run by Rebecca Lukens, one of the first women to lead a major industrial company (she led the mill for 25 years).[16] However, during more recent times, as the steel industry declined, so did the city of Coatesville. Today what remains of the mill is owned by Cleveland-Cliffs, Inc.

Coatesville, in many ways, is an anomaly in Chester County. The contrast is striking. Chester County is one of the wealthiest counties in PA whereas Coatesville is the county's most impoverished community—30% of its population live below the poverty line.[17] Chester County's population of 522,000 is 78.9% white (7.5% Latino, 5.7% Black/African American, 5.6% Asian) while Coatesville, a city with a population of 13,000, is 45.3%

Black/African American (25.9% white, 24.5% Latino).[18] Chester County is known for its rolling hills, winding creeks, and picturesque stone homes, barns, and fences. Horse farms still exist among the rapidly expanding suburban McMansion neighborhoods. The area was made famous through the paintings of Andrew Wyeth along with historical events such as the Revolutionary War's Battle of Brandywine. Meanwhile, Coatesville, the only city in Chester County, is the opposite. Withered structures dot its main street along with corroded steel structures from the once burgeoning steel mill which remind visitors of a time-gone-by when the steel industry was king. Coatesville shares many socio-economic challenges characteristic of larger urban communities which are in stark contrast to the rest of the county.

Over the years, racial tensions have erupted. One of the most problematic racial events in Coatesville's history involved the lynching of Zachariah Walker in 1911 that cast a shadow over the community for decades.[19] In the 1980s, black steel workers, including my father, filed a class action lawsuit against Lukens Steel Company for racial discrimination in hiring and promotions.[20] Coatesville Area High School which is a majority minority district has had its share of racial incidents too.[21] I briefly highlight a portion of Coatesville's history as a point of reference to situate my experience within that complicated history which is a small milestone within the larger African American history. Reflecting back on that pivotal high school football moment, I grew up that day walking off that practice field—I left behind the naiveté of childhood and entered the reality of being black in America.

Although I was disappointed at the time, when I began to take on leadership positions in academe, I relied heavily on my experiences in sports and the responsibility of playing QB. As a QB, you learn to prepare, to work, to sacrifice, to study, to perfect your foot work, and your throwing motion. In the process, you learn the strengths and weaknesses of the players around you and how to make them successful. For example, I remember one of our running backs would always get confused about which side of the center to run when taking the hand off when running the fullback (FB) trap. In our option offense, the FB trap was a quick FB run up the middle as the quarterback made a quick reverse pivot hand off to the FB. If either player went to the wrong side of the center (based upon the strength of the formation), they would run into each other in a thunderous collision. Needless to say, we smacked into each other a few times. When we had a moment, I asked him why he was running to the wrong side on the play. He acknowledged he was unsure which side to run to. So I told him, if the play was going to the center's right side, I would tap my right thigh before I took the snap, and if the play was going to the center's left side, I would tap my left thigh before taking the snap. Then, I said, he would always know what side to run. Once I did that, it ended any miscues with the hand off. It's a simple example, but it underscores how effective leaders can assist in helping individuals become more successful in the tasks they have to complete.

The leadership skills I learned in sports I use every day in my leadership positions such as department chair. What applied in one realm was transferable to the other. Just like a QB, a department chair has to be prepared, has to work, has to sacrifice, and has to learn the strengths and weakness of the people he or she leads and learn how to put them in the best position to succeed. And just like a QB, when the team is having success, the leader receives a lot of accolades, but when the team is not doing well, the leader gets all the blame. So although, that day in 1985 was devastating, I did go on to use the skills that I learned in football throughout my career. As the old saying goes, I was able to "turn that scar into a star."

After finishing my senior year at Coatesville, I focused on transitioning to West Chester University. When I arrived on the University campus in the fall 1987, I thought I was ready for college, until I realized how much I needed to improve as a student. I also found some professors, such as my second basic writing teacher were supportive, while others, such as my Spanish teacher were not. I still remember the note my Spanish teacher wrote on one of my Spanish tests on which I did poorly. In bold, red ink he wrote, "You should drop the course, before it's too late!" To this day, I don't use red ink or red font to correct student papers. Instead of teaching us how to learn Spanish, the teacher expected us to learn it ourselves. The problem was the teacher did not give us strategies or ways to learn the material. It was all conversational. He would make statements in English, and we had to say the phrase in Spanish. As he called on individuals and stated the English sentence, he would wait a second or two for the Spanish answer. His teaching approach caused A LOT of anxiety as he went faster and faster from person to person. I can still hear him saying, "I give you the book." "He gives her the book." "She gives him the book," etc. He would pause for an answer. If you didn't know the answer, he would move on to the next student. His teaching style did not match my learning style. I wasn't fast enough to simultaneously translate the English words into Spanish, change the syntax or pronounce them in Spanish. I was striking out on all levels. One time I answered, "I don't know." He paused, looked at me and said, "At least say it in Spanish. Say, 'Yo no se.'" In an entire semester of Spanish 1, "Yo no se" was the only Spanish I learned. To this day, it's one of the few Spanish phrases I know. Later, when my kids were taking Spanish, I would somehow work in my limited knowledge with "Yo no se" to their amusement. It's funny now, but it was painful then.

The benefit of having to struggle is you become more savvy towards obstacles and how to overcome them. As you overcome one obstacle after another, you learn to be resourceful. Being resourceful is an excellent leadership trait and it helped me immensely as a department chair. With resourcefulness, when confronted with an obstacle, the obstacle doesn't become debilitating or insurmountable. You can rely on experience in navigating the impediment. I became very good at finding ways to succeed despite the challenges. For example, when I was a graduate student, I didn't own a computer. However, there was a computer in the office of the faculty member who I served as a graduate assistant. Since the faculty member trusted me, he gave me a key to the office. Therefore, I was able to use the computer when the faculty member was not there. Typically, the office was consistently available on Friday late afternoons and on the weekends. Thus, Friday late afternoons and Saturday mornings became the time when I would complete my assignments and papers.

One late Friday afternoon, I was in the office using the computer to complete a paper. At the time, the Department of Communication Studies and the Department of History occupied offices on the fifth floor of Main Hall with the respective departmental main offices in opposite corners of the building. The office I was working in was a corner office, so when I was working at the computer, I could see the History Department's main office at the opposite end of the hallway as well as the elevators that were directly outside of my door. Dr. Irene Shur, a long-time History professor who founded the Holocaust Studies Program at WCU (and was one of the longest serving faculty members in the PA State System), had a very distinctive walk. She always wore shoes with a slight heel that made a click-clacking sound as she walked. She was a short, round woman with olive skin, dark hair, a few freckles, and piercing dark eyes. She often carried a briefcase. When she spoke her deep, baritone voice commanded authority. When she walked down the hallway, I could tell it was her by the rhythmic sound of her shoes.

On this day, I heard her footsteps walking down the hallway, the noise getting louder as she neared my corner office. Then, all of a sudden, the footsteps stopped. I looked up and there was Dr. Irene Shur in my office doorway.

Dr. Shur: "Young man, who are you?"

Me: "I'm Tim Brown, I'm Dr. Pearson's graduate assistant."

Dr. Shur: "Young man, I'm not sure what your plans are, but I see you being very successful and working in academe. I can see you working with students and students will enjoy taking your courses. Keep up the good work!"

As soon as Dr. Shur finished speaking, she left and caught the elevator to leave the building. Interestingly, I never had a conversation with Dr. Shur before or after that moment. At the time, it was the word of encouragement that I needed because I wasn't sure where my graduate studies were going. Dr. Shur's words and vision were inspiring! I was honored that she would take the time to speak into my life. Looking back I can see how her prophetic words foreshadowed my successful career in academe. I have taught and mentored a multitude of students who have enjoyed me as a teacher and faculty member.

Thinking back to that moment, if someone would have told me I would have a successful career in higher education, I would have said that person was crazy. Consider that as an undergraduate, I was on academic probation after my first semester but would improve my GPA and earn an internship at Fox29 Philadelphia. After graduation, I would work for my hometown newspaper. I would return to WCU as a graduate assistant, go on to Ohio University on a graduate assistantship and be the first in my class at Ohio University to complete my dissertation and land a tenure-track position at Buffalo State College. Then, I would get recruited back to WCU by the same department chair (Denny) who encouraged me to pursue an M.A. and then a Ph.D. Next, I would succeed Denny as department chair, serving ten years while creating WCU's Faculty Mentoring Program and the Multicultural Faculty Commission, along with serving as the Chair of Chairs and the Special Assistant to the Provost. All this from my roots as a first-generation African American student, son of a steel worker from Coatesville, PA! It's an improbable and amazing journey!

Dr. Irene Shur gave me the initial boost to continue down the academic path and I followed that academic path which would eventually lead to more opportunities. As I continued with my studies, I started to think about getting my Ph.D. Working with the WCU professors had given me a sense of what a faculty member does and by getting to know them, I realized they were regular people. My professor suggested that if I wanted to pursue my Ph.D., I should write a master's thesis rather than complete my degree the non-thesis route. My confidence had risen so much, I agreed. Our Communication Studies master's program was recently created, only one or two students had graduated from the program and no one had completed a master's thesis.

Since I had an interest in sports and I had developed an interest in the study of rhetoric (how messages persuade), I stumbled upon my thesis topic. I was writing a paper in which I was analyzing the rhetoric of President Jimmy Carter and came across information about President Carter persuading a number of countries to boycott the 1980 Summer Olympics although he did not have the power over the U.S. Olympic Committee to do so. It was an interesting fact that I didn't know. The thesis idea would be to analyze how Present Carter used rhetoric to convince not only the U.S. but other countries to boycott the 1980 Olympic Games when he did not have the authority to make that decision. My professor liked the idea and my thesis project was born.

At some point, as I was analyzing various speeches by President Carter, I made a particular claim about what was occurring in one of his speeches. My advisor suggested that in order to support my claim, I'd have to personally ask Jimmy Carter if it was true.

Undaunted, I took him up on his suggestion, writing President Carter a letter with my questions. Amazingly the President was a guest speaker on our campus that semester, so I asked a faculty member to give the President my letter and the initial draft of my work. About a month later, I received a personal letter from the President answering my questions. The first part of his letter still impresses me, "To Tim Brown. I have read your research paper with care and found it to be the best analysis of the 1980 Olympics issue that I have read."[22] Wow! Not bad for a kid from Coatesville who struggled with writing and was on academic probation his first semester in college. The letter was a turning point in my academic career. It showed I could write and conduct salient research that could contribute to the field of Communication Studies.

I remember showing the letter to my professor and to Denny and they were ecstatic! They praised me over and over. In fact, Denny displayed a copy of my letter and President Carter's response outside the main office. I remember Denny just beaming — "Oh man, the kid from Coatesville! The kid from Coatesville!" I would become the first student to complete a master's thesis in the department, and I would become the first African American male to complete the program.

What I came to appreciate about struggle was it gave me great insight and empathy as a leader. I couldn't assume just by looking at someone what struggles he or she had to endure or overcome.

My experiences as an African American man gave me an emotional intelligence few leaders had. I saw my role as assisting students navigate the system by being helpful and inspirational. You lead as you would like to be led. Before I became department chair, my thought was if I ever became chair, I would be the chair I always wanted as a student and as a faculty member. Too many leaders have forgotten the struggle, have forgotten what it is like to be cast aside, to be an outsider, to be an afterthought. If there was anything I was good at, it was building relationships and learning people's strengths and weaknesses in order to give them the opportunity to succeed. Let me be clear: Giving someone the opportunity to succeed and being successful are not the same thing. For example, I was given the opportunity to pursue graduate school, but it was up to me to succeed. Effective leadership provides opportunities and support to enable others to succeed. As a leader, I have done the same for others based upon the examples set by my mentors. No struggle, no challenge, no roadblock can upend a person who has opportunity and support.

Chapter 4: You Can't Make People "Do Right"

My parents' wisdom is something I will always cherish. Although they didn't have college degrees, they are the most perceptive people I know because they gained great knowledge from their life circumstances. They are versed on many subjects and could size up a situation better than anyone I knew. They have strong morals as well as faith and carried themselves with character and dignity. They "talked the talk and walked the walk."

What I also appreciated when I became older and had my own family was how they endured despite the racism and societal challenges they faced. My mother was the most positive and pleasant person I knew. She cared a great deal about her family, friends, and people in general. She loved to laugh, and I found laughter was a great coping mechanism. But don't cross her. She was quick with her wit and tongue—she had no problem "setting someone straight," if she needed to. I can still hear her say, "You needed that like a hole in the head!" "You couldn't leave well enough alone!" "Don't make me get out of this chair!" and my favorite, "Get *it* together!" And as she grew older, she became more emboldened. When there was some offense, she felt compelled to say something about it. That was my mom; she was a fighter to the end. My dad, on the other hand, is the calm one who typically does not call attention to himself. He is very perceptive of people and gets along with everyone. He is the model of consistency, commitment, and a strong work ethic. He takes life in stride and is reserved in most situations. But if something did bother him, he could speak forcibly and with authority.

When I was younger there was a family who lived next to us, a single mom and her grown son. The grown son had two kids and sometimes they would come over to play with us and the other neighborhood kids. One day we were playing a game called "King of the Hill" in our yard and then a game called "Pile On." In "Pile On," you had two rows of kids on hands and knees facing one another. If there were eight kids, there would be two lines of four facing one another. One person would whisper in the ear of each player who to pile on. Typically, everyone was given the same name except for the person to be piled on who was given a different name. When the command "go" was given, the person who everyone was piling on would get pummeled from the weight of the pile.

That day when we were playing "Pile On," the grown son's kids came over to play and one of them was the person to be piled on. The kid was also a talker. So after he ended up on the bottom of the pile, he started trash talking. The next time, I was the person to be piled on. I took it, but for some reason, the kid was still popping off about being piled on. What was a good-natured game between kids became more aggressive and rough. I didn't appreciate him coming into our backyard and creating hostility. We exchanged words. He stepped into my face. The next thing I know I punched him square in the nose. There was silence as he grabbed his nose. When he opened his hands, there was blood running from his nose. He grabbed his nose and ran home. The kids began laughing. I don't think we ever played with or saw them again after the incident.

I think frustration had built up in me because the next-door kids tended to roughhouse and create arguments. My reaction was a culmination of their antics when they would come over to play. When I think about the incident, however, it reminds me of what my mother used to say: "You can't make people do right." As leaders, we can lead the way, we can tell people what we expect, but we can't control how others act. We can only control how we react. This is an important lesson of leadership. As a leader, you can set the example; you can be a servant-leader; you can set the tone for how to complete tasks, show people how to sacrifice, and how to treat one another, but at the end of the day the other people you lead have to catch the vision. Leaders can't make people "do right." We can only lead them in what they should do.

Over the years, this was a hard lesson to learn because some faculty members are examples of what not to do. From my experience, most faculty members would have at least one aspect of their job that would set them off. It might be the time and/or the days of the classes they were assigned to teach, what they were teaching, the number of preps, the amount of professional development money they received. . . the list goes on and on. As the years progressed, so did the frequency of the asinine whining of some faculty. By my tenth year as department chair, I knew it was time to move on to something else as the faculty laments became more and more ridiculous—such as some faculty members complaining about having to come to campus to teach three days week. If these faculty had to work a real job where they didn't have job security, where they had to hustle, where they had to sacrifice for the good of the organization while also being amiable toward their co-workers, it might change their attitude about working on a college campus.

When I was a faculty member, I observed few faculty members working beyond the minimum. Too many were and are out of touch with today's economy, blissfully unaware of the job insecurity of most Americans or how many Americans work more hours with stagnant pay and pitiful health insurance. Even the current pandemic reinforces how privileged faculty are since they can work remotely and still receive a paycheck.

Yet, in ten years as department chair, I never lost my cool, and I only raised my voice twice. I definitely identified with President Obama when he was in office—how people would carry on and berate him, yet he always carried himself with dignity and class, when I'm sure he felt like cursing people out. Obama was a good role model for me. I could relate to him as another black man in leadership who had to deal with people who had no shame about how they acted.

But no matter who the leader is, there will be people who will not do the right thing. I once had an adjunct faculty member (we'll call the person "Joe") who complained to me about his schedule for the upcoming semester. Keep in mind that Joe had a good salary with excellent benefits. Plus, he didn't have the extra responsibilities of a tenure-track employee (such as advising, research, committee work, etc.) and only taught at night which was his preference. All Joe had to do was teach four courses for a full-time salary. However, he complained because he was scheduled to teach Tuesday and Thursday evenings (two three-hour classes on Tuesday and two three-hour classes on Thursday). The complaint—he wanted to complete a non-teaching project and needed Thursdays as a travel day instead of a teaching day. I explained to the person I had 40 people to schedule, and I could not accommodate everyone's personal requests. I suggested that Joe explore alternative ways to finish the project. Eventually, the complaint went to the associate dean to "resolve it." I told the associate dean my perspective—if I started making these types of allowances, other faculty would demand to have their schedules changed as well. Needless to say, the associate dean changed the adjunct faculty member's schedule to Monday and Tuesday nights. Ironically, the project Joe was complaining he wanted to accomplish never materialized, but he did get to work only the first two nights of the week as a full-time adjunct.

Over the years, one document I became especially familiar with as a chair was our faculty collective bargaining agreement (CBA) which set the rules for the university faculty. Unfortunately, the rules which provide clarity also allow faculty to do the minimum because everyone gets paid on a predetermined scale. There is no incentive for individuals to do an exceptional job. As a result, the ones who are conscientious tend to do more work—work that the minimalists don't give a damn about. Need someone to cover an Open House Day on Saturday morning? Not the minimalists. Need someone to serve as a judge for a speech tournament on a Friday afternoon? Not the minimalists. Need someone to observe a fellow faculty member for review? Not the minimalists. In addition to the minimalists, you also have the incompetents. You can assign the work but it won't get done in a timely manner or correctly or it might not get done at all. For example, the person might observe a faculty member but never write up and turn in the observation. This list goes on and on, and it is allowed to persist because there is absolutely zero accountability.

During my time as a department chair, I also found incompetence was tolerated. When we needed a new department secretary instead of allowing us to interview candidates to determine the person's skill-level, the dean moved someone from another unit (which was being phased out) into our department. However, it soon became apparent that the assigned secretary could not complete the duties for the position.

Not having a competent secretary was compounded by the size of our department. Although we had over 500 majors and 40+ faculty members, we were the only department of our size with only one secretary. A lot of "balls were dropped" during this period. It was difficult because I'm a perfectionist, and I don't like errors. However, to get a different secretary, I had to allow her to screw things up and then document her incompetence. Quickly, the faculty began to notice. "Tim, my schedule had me listed for four courses; now I'm only listed for two." "Tim, my independent study is built incorrectly; it's listed at one credit when it should be three." "Tim, my classes are now missing." I also received a series of emails from students, "Dr. Brown, I was enrolled in two COM 499 classes, but when I attempted to swap out of one into a different class, I was dropped from both sections." On and on it went, error after error. I kept complaining to the dean (who never owned up to the mistake of placing the person into our department). The best I could do was get the person transferred into another department. Thankfully, another department had two secretaries, one was the primary secretary and the other one was the greeter. When the greeter position became available, I was able to have our person moved into the other department. I was pleased when the transfer occurred but looking back on that moment what a bizarre way to run an organization!

These are just a few examples that illustrate you can't make people do right. In contrast, there will be many people who will catch the vision and will follow the leader's philosophy. When people catch the global vision—it makes for great synergy and in the case of higher education, the students are better served. As a leader, all you can do is set the standard in work ethic, sacrifice, integrity and collegiality. When you do this, your organization and the people in it will be better off. But at the end of the day, all you can do is lead by example. You can't make people "do right!"

#14 High School Football (1986)

My parents (circa 2000)

MY DISSERTATION DEFENSE (WHEN I RECEIVED MY DOCTORATE FROM OHIO UNIVERSITY, 1997-JW SMITH FAR RIGHT)

National Communication Association (NCA) presentation, 1996

Chapter 5: "All My Skinfolk Ain't Kinfolk"

It's interesting how many shows, films, and events are remakes of remakes. One example is Planet of the Apes. I remember vaguely from when I was a kid some of the original films and battles between humans and an evolved ape species. The more recent reboot of the series in addition to having superior special effects and action, also provides critical insights into leadership. For example, one scene in *Dawn of the Planet of the Apes*[23] illustrates how leaders must always be perceptive and wary of people, especially people who are supposed to be on their side.

Without retelling the entire story, *Dawn of the Planet of the Apes* takes place ten years after a pandemic, "Simian Flu," wipes out most of the human population. While the Simian Flu has a devastating effect on humans, the virus bolsters the intelligence of the primates left on Earth. The primates are led by a chimpanzee named Caesar. Under Caesar's leadership the group builds a

71

community in a forest in Northern, California outside of San Francisco. Their community becomes alarmed, however, when humans are found in the forest searching for a hydroelectric dam to fix and restore power to the city.

As Caesar attempts to manage the breach of their territory, another chimpanzee, Koba, grows bitter towards Caesar. From an audience member's perspective, you can understand why Caesar is being cautious towards the humans. However, Koba does not have that perspective, does not "see" the big picture and only wants his way—which is to fight the humans. Koba is resentful because he was experimented on when he was in a research lab and he wants revenge on the humans. He dislikes Caesar's leadership and grows increasingly hostile arguing that Caesar is weak towards the humans because he was raised by a human. In contrast, Caesar explains to the group that fighting the humans would lead to the chimpanzee's destruction. He reminds the primates that the humans have too many weapons. Caesar argues that working for peace with the humans is better than fighting against them. Fighting would destroy them all.

The more Caesar tries to keep the peace, the more infuriated Koba becomes. Koba agitates the other primates, convincing them to support his position. Eventually, Koba goes from being a discontent to plotting Caesar's demise. One night while Caesar is high in a tree looking over the territory, Koba shoots Caesar with a stolen weapon. Caesar plummets from the tree and is assumed dead while Koba takes control of the group by announcing Caesar has been shot by a human. Now, the entire group is whipped into a frenzy. Koba gets the war he wants as he calls on avenging Caesar's death by fighting the humans. Koba's desire to murder Caesar is ironic on many levels. Earlier in the film, for example, when Koba confronted Caesar, Caesar had the opportunity to kill Koba. Caesar, however, stated the Ape principle—"Apes don't kill other Apes"—so he spared Koba's life.

While *Dawn of the Planet of the Apes* is a rebooted science-fiction film that has mass appeal, the situations depicted have broad application beyond entertainment—especially as they relate to leadership. The scene of Koba taking over the leadership of the group (albeit short-lived) illustrates many important lessons for leaders. After all, what leader hasn't experienced what happened to Caesar—being targeted by one of your own people! Caesar being shot by a disgruntled group member who was acting on faulty information and perspective is an irony of leadership. To make matters worse, Koba after shooting Caesar blames it on someone else. This scene is a perfect metaphor for how problem faculty will challenge the leader, cause strife, then blame others for the conflict. Leaders have to realize they will be a target in large part due to individuals not seeing the big picture, not sharing the vision, and going to any lengths to get their way even if it means causing mass causalities.

Many important principles can be unpacked from this scene as it relates to leadership. Principle #1: Any leader is a target. Although Caesar had the good of the group in mind when he was leading, others found fault with his leadership. When it comes to leadership, it is impossible to please everyone. Anytime a leader has to make a decision someone will be pleased while others will be dissatisfied. Effective leaders will not base their decisions on the happiness of individuals; instead they will use specific values when making their decisions. In my case, the primary value I used was how the decision would benefit the students and the program.

No matter how well you do your job, how many people you help, how generous you are with your time, how charitable you are in allocating resources, how well you are completing your tasks, how effective you are at fixing problems, and meeting all due dates, some people will criticize you. If the leader, however, consistently applies a set of values to make decisions (such as does the action best support our students or program), some individuals might not like the decision, but at least the leader can point to the value upon which the decision was based. Individuals might still argue, but the leader can remind them of the value involved and how it relates to the big picture. It's up to the person to embrace the vision, not for the leader to make the person happy.

There are plenty of examples of organizations achieving accomplishments over the personal happiness of the individuals in the group. One of the most noteworthy examples is the Pittsburgh Steelers of the 1970s. The Steelers are considered one of football's greatest dynasties, winning four Super Bowls in four appearances in the 1970s with 18 members of the team such as Terry Bradshaw, Franco Harris, Mean Joe Greene, Jack Lambert, and their head coach, Chuck Noll, enshrined in the Hall of Fame. The Steelers achieved greatness despite not everyone being "happy" with how the team was led.

In football, one of the most important relationships on the team is the bond between the head coach and the quarterback. On the Steelers dynasty team, however, the relationship between the head coach Chuck Noll and QB Terry Bradshaw was not the greatest—both men had strong opinions and perspectives for how the team should be run. At times Noll was hard on Bradshaw, but from a coaching standpoint, Noll's job was not to make Bradshaw happy. Instead, his job was to get the most out of Bradshaw, to elevate his play, and to hold him accountable. Bradshaw, who won four Super Bowls under Noll, resented Noll and his coaching style.[24] However, by embracing the greater vision (winning championships), they achieved more by focusing on the overall goal rather than individual happiness. I'm sure if Noll had attempted to keep everyone on the team happy, the Steelers might not have achieved the greatness they did.

Principle #2: Don't underestimate the lengths a person will go to get their own way. In the scene described earlier, Koba was so angry he was unconcerned with the consequences of his actions. Many primates died because he was blinded by his own desires. The same occurs in organizations. The "bad apples" don't care about the vision, can't grasp all the leader is accomplishing, and will only interpret the situation from their own selfish point of view. The problem is "bad apples" are not concerned about collateral damage; they want their way regardless. And the damage that can be done by these individuals is far reaching and irreversible.

One of the best examples of individuals pushing for their own way and causing irreversible collateral damage involved a faculty member and a course we were offering as part of the general education curriculum. The person was redesigning the course based upon personal preference (to spend less time on campus) as opposed to designing a course that was in the best interest of the program. What began as one faculty member's selfish ambition eventually caused an internal split in the department over the course itself and whether the department should even be teaching it. Some faculty were more concerned about their niche area of research than about the discipline's contribution to general education.

Principle #3: Don't be surprised if the person targeting you is one of your own kind. Caesar might not have thought he would be taken down by another chimp, but it happened. Likewise, as a leader you might share similarities with others by race, gender, etc. but sharing these similarities does not mean that person will be an ally. In these cases, it's really perplexing to watch self-absorbed people, and those who support them, suck the life out of organizations. Instead of focusing on ways to engage students, and to fulfill the needs of the department (such as being a faculty advisor to a student group, teaching a graduate course, serving on a department committee, etc.), a few people attempted to spend as little time as possible in the classroom and on campus.

As a leader, you must evaluate the people around you, give them honest and constructive feedback, and give them the support they need to acquire any missing skills. A leader must be perceptive of who is and who isn't aligned with the vision and who is and isn't aligned with the leader. Talent evaluation along with perceiving people's character is an important skill. When advising students, I would explain that everyone brings joy to my office—some bring joy when they enter, and others bring joy when they leave. Be the person who brings joy when you enter!

I once heard an excerpt of a sermon by T.J. Jakes in which he discussed how different types of people help others reach their destiny.[25] Two types of people he described in his sermon stood out to me—the "confidant" and the "constituent." Both are necessary for a leader to accomplish the goals of the organization but each has a different role/function.

The constituent is a person who is for the leader's agenda but not necessarily for the leader. Thus, a constituent will support the ideas and initiatives that he or she also agrees with. As a leader, you must not confuse the support of the constituent as personal support. Rather, if the constituent likes the agenda, he or she will support it. If the leader would like to take an action or initiative that is not an agenda the constituent can get behind, the constituent will not support it. For example, the person might be a team player when it comes to completing organizational tasks, but if a problem arises and the leader would like the person to speak up at a meeting or to present an opposing viewpoint, the constituent will not embrace the request as it is not part of his or her personal agenda. It might be expressed as, "I'm here to teach the courses you need, but I'm not going to explain in a department meeting why it's important everyone should take turns teaching graduate courses."

Constituents are necessary for moving the organizational agenda forward and for getting organizational tasks done, but they only personally support the leader when it's in their best interests. Sometimes leaders get this mixed up and are taken aback, or surprised, or offended when a constituent will not personally support the leader. In reality, it is the leader who has it mixed up. The constituent never personally supported the leader—it was the agenda that was being supported. If the leader is replaced or if there is another agenda that aligns with the constituent, the constituent will pursue that agenda.

The confidant, on the other hand, has the leader's back no matter what—even if it means telling the leader right from wrong. The confidant is not afraid to offer opposing points of view, but he or she always speaks highly of the leader to others; the confidant is not a back stabber or gossiper. A confidant is a true friend and always wants the best for the leader. If you are in an organization, most likely a confidant is not someone in your unit. Being outside the unit gives the confidant better insight and perspective. Confidants have no self-interest in the unit other than supporting the leader and helping the leader succeed.

Confidants are necessary for leaders as they see the leader as a person who has wants, desires, and feelings. Confidants are individuals who have great character and have deep institutional knowledge. Confidants keep the leader balanced and can process information and situations from another perspective. In my own case, I was fortunate to have several confidants I could meet with, talk to, and work though the issues of leading a large department. These individuals were genuine and supportive confidants who I could rely on when I needed perspective or support. Their wisdom was/is greatly appreciated.

The bottom line is there are no "natural" allies. Leaders must be excellent readers of people and their character. Leaders must keep a functional "distance" from their colleagues. This doesn't mean the leader is unfriendly—it means the leader should not give the appearance of hanging out with only certain people in the unit and not others. If you are making time to meet with people, then everyone should have the same opportunity. When I was a faculty member, I made it a point to have lunch with Denny at least once a year to discuss my goals with him, to keep him updated on my work, and to receive feedback. As department chair, I continued that process by giving all tenure-track faculty members an opportunity to meet with me to keep me updated on their growth and development as faculty members. It was a great way to build rapport, to get a sense of their goals, and to connect them with other faculty or resources.

I learned the lesson of building relationships very well from my time as a graduate student at WCU and later at Ohio University. In fact, when I arrived at Ohio University in the fall of 1994, it was a brand-new environment in which to test what I learned at that point in my career. From previous visits to the campus and talking to a few graduate students and faculty, I knew some people, but I didn't know anyone well. I had to start the process of relationship building. One of the most important bonds a graduate student has is with his or her dissertation advisor.

I had the opportunity to work with a few rhetoric faculty in the department, but I had to determine who was the best fit. I don't remember when I first encountered Dr. J.W. Smith—it might have been at the opening meeting in Lasher Hall—but after being in the program and having the opportunity to talk to him and to take a course with him, I liked his style. I liked how student-centered he was. When I made an appointment with him, I made sure to have my pitch for my dissertation topic ready. Once I mentioned my topic, J.W. stopped me and said, "The best dissertation is a done dissertation!" That sold me right there! Once I made J.W. my dissertation advisor, we would have many meetings where we discussed revisions for my dissertation. In time, a place called Miller's Chicken in Athens, Ohio would become our dissertation meeting place.

Miller's sold the best and biggest fried chicken wings—ever! The wings were like turkey wings, and the price was right. The food was very inexpensive, something like four wings (drumette and wingette) for $8.00. We would get wings, fries, and Snapple. Miller's became our once a week go to spot—it became a home away from home. After discussing dissertation revisions, we talked politics, sports, music, NCA (our National Communication Association conference) and various other topics. And we would always have two or three good laughs along the way. At the time I didn't realize it, but J.W. was pouring into me not only his wisdom but his friendship. I appreciated the time J.W. sacrificed for me and the sense of community he created for me. I had lived my entire life in Coatesville or West Chester in Chester County, Pennsylvania and Athens, Ohio was a long way from home and a different environment. The time spent with J.W. Smith built community for me, a community that eventually expanded to include my wife Laura, our church family of Adullam Ministries, Pam and Wesley Dykes, and other graduate students of color such as Rex Crawley, Katrina Bell, and Jeff Tyus along with the forensic team graduate assistants. With J.W.'s guidance, he directed me through the dissertation process. To this day, when I'm meeting with students interested in completing a thesis or dissertation, I still use J.W.'s advice, "The best dissertation is a done dissertation!"

Some 20 years later, I had a student working as my communication assistant when I was department chair which evolved into a Miller's moment. A graduate student in our program desired to pursue his Ph.D., and I needed someone to manage the D2L site for the major which involved forwarding messages, updating the calendar, posting information from student groups, and editing my monthly chair messages. Having the graduate student as the communication assistant was a great way to keep our undergraduate students informed but also gave the graduate student a perspective on faculty life. In time, our weekly meetings moved from my office to Timothy's Restaurant in West Chester. Timothy's became our Miller's. I was preparing the graduate student as I was prepared 20 years ago.

I began this chapter by referring to the sci-fi film *Dawn of the Planet of the Apes* to illustrate several leadership principles that are relevant for any leader. Leadership, while rewarding, does not come without its challenges. Leaders must be very discerning of people, their motives, and their character. As a leader, you might not be able to stop those who plot against you, but, unlike Caesar, you can avoid getting shot out of a tree!

Chapter 6: Mascot

When I was a student, one of the books I enjoyed reading was the *Autobiography of Malcolm X*. One idea that resonated with me was when he discussed being a mascot. When Malcolm X's mother had a mental breakdown, she was placed in a state mental hospital, and he was sent to a foster home in Michigan. While he was treated fairly by the white couple who looked after him, he understood from his day-to-day interactions with them and his white classmates that he was not treated as a person but rather as a thing, a pet—a mascot.

> What I am trying to say is that it just never dawned upon them that I could, that I wasn't a pet, but a human being. They didn't give me credit for having the same sensitivity, intellect, and understanding that they would have been ready and willing to recognize in a white boy in my position. But it has historically been the case with white people, in their regard for black people, that even though we might be *with* them, we weren't considered *of* them. Even though they appeared to have opened

the door, it was still closed. Thus they never did really see *me*.[26]

Malcolm X's comments resonate! As blacks aspire and continue to break barriers and take on leadership positions, we are constantly cast in the role of the mascot. Malcom X pointedly articulated the paradox of black life—as doors open we might be *with* the dominate culture but we are not considered *of* them. Very few times do others really see us.

Being the mascot is like breathing. When we breathe, we don't think about breathing until something hinders our ability to breathe. Likewise, being a mascot is not something you think about until something occurs that reminds you of your blackness. These microaggressions that occur from time-to-time mimic cold water being poured down your back—they instantly gain your attention. Any African American can recall the first moment when he or she came to fully understand that he or she was the other—the mascot. Mine occurred when I was about 4 or 5 years old. My first best friend lived a couple doors down the street from me. I remember I would go over to his house to play. He had an assortment of matchbox cars, army men, Legos, etc. that we would play with. I always had a good time at his house. One day we were in his yard and I can't recall the game, but something occurred, and we began to argue. The next thing I knew he called me the N word and I called him a honky—then it was on! I remember punching him in the chest, while he grabbed and held onto me. His grandmother heard the commotion and told us to stop fighting. I remember walking home thinking about what he said.

In recalling that moment, it's interesting how two kids who had shown no animosity towards one another could suddenly hurl hurtful words at one another. While my friend and I would get over that incident—we remained good friends through elementary school before he moved away—the moment stayed with me as it was the first time I was aware others first saw me through my blackness. Although I saw myself as myself, I was now aware others did not see me as I saw myself. And as I grew, I came to understand most individuals would see me through my blackness. To my parents' credit, I was raised to consider myself to be just as good as anyone else, but in the back of my mind, I was aware others might perceive me differently due to my race/ethnicity.

It was part of life. You learn to navigate it. For example, I remember when I was a graduate student at Ohio University and one professor constantly confused me with another student of color— the classic "they all look alike." Yet, I didn't look anything like the other student—my skin tone was brown whereas the other graduate student was light in complexion. I had a close haircut, he had wavy brown hair. I didn't wear glasses, while he did. We had so many differences in appearance, yet the faculty member would always confuse us and call us by the wrong name. It might not be a seismic example, but it illustrates how white folks tend to not see us. It served as a reminder of our blackness through our daily interactions and encounters.

Despite having success in one's career, I believe being a mascot is always in the back of a black person's mind. Although I had many accomplishments as a faculty member and department chair, I sometimes wondered whether I was being selected for my skills and abilities or if I was being selected for appearances. In the presence of others, I became perceptive to power dynamics. I would observe who other folks sat next to, who they talked to, the nature of their conversation, the inside jokes, who was being joked about, and who got the jokes. I would observe how people related to me, what they said (or did not say). These observations can reveal all you need to know about who is and isn't part of the club.

There are always mascot moments in one's life. Another pivotal example of the mascot occurred in the spring of 2017, when there was a call for an Interim Dean of the College of Arts and Humanities at WCU. Given my career and accomplishments, I had everything one would want in a dean. I rose through the ranks, achieving tenure and promotion to full professor in 2007, served 10 years as department chair for one of the largest departments on campus, and I was a stellar teacher and advisor. I maintained an active research agenda with publications, conference presentations, and speaking engagements. I was elected/appointed to prominent

committees on campus from the Tenure and Promotion Committee, to the Curriculum and Academic Policies Council, to the University Budget Committee and I served as the Chair of Chairs and
Special Assistant to the Provost. Also, I had been honored with a
slew of awards such as the Martin Luther King Drum Major for Justice Award and receiving recognition from the WCU Board of Trus-
tees. In my discipline, I served in many roles for the Eastern Communication Association including the role of Second Vice-President.
In addition, I was one of the few (if not the only) African American
males who was a full professor and served as a department chair
on campus. Furthermore, I was a local product, a first-generation
college student who earned B.A. and M.A. degrees from WCU—my
background was Horatio Algeresque.

Needless to say, I wasn't selected for the position. The accomplishments, leadership experience, and being an African American
faculty member with strong interpersonal skills—simply did not
matter. I was a mascot. I wasn't part of the club. As Malcolm X said,
"I was *with* them but not considered *of* them." I shouldn't have
been surprised. That's how the story goes—an all too familiar one
for African Americans in the academy.[27] It's no different for other
African Americans across the spectrum in other careers and profes-
sions. In the spring of 2017, WCU was telling me to "shut up and
dribble."

While the game hasn't changed, the communities marginalized people construct to inoculate themselves from an oppressive society has not changed either. African Americans, since arriving in the Americas, have constructed a culture where we are valued and understood. We have created a culture that reaffirms our humanity, experiences, and cultural ways of communicating. From my experiences, there is something energizing when a group of African Americans come together. Scholar bell hooks called these spaces the "homeplace." The homeplace is a created environment based upon care and nurturance that reaffirms African Americans' humanity in the face of oppression.[28] The homeplace operates as a place of resistance, where Blacks are understood, where we don't have to explain ourselves, where our practices and lived experiences are the norm, and where we are valued and supported. In the homeplace, we are free to be—to communicate and relate to one another in African American stylistic ways of communication. Rickford and Rickford further defined the ways in which African Americans relate to and communicate with one another as, "Spoken Soul," which captures the dynamic and interwoven tapestry of language, culture, identity, and lived experience.[29]

My fascination with African American ways of communicating led me as a graduate student to works by Geneva Smitherman, Jack Daniels, Mel Cummings, Ron Jackson, and Thomas Kochman. It became an area of research I contributed to often. I wrote articles reflecting my interests in sports, Black masculinity, and communication focusing on figures from Allen Iverson to Donovan McNabb to LeBron James.[30] In addition, I wrote about the intersections of these areas with popular culture as I completed articles on subjects from Tupac Shakur to the film *Barbershop.*[31] It's like the old saying, research is often "me research." I was learning about myself and my cultural identity in addition to making sense of how I communicated. More importantly, through my research, I was able to identify the intersectionality of African American cultural values and how they shaped communication practices. Over time, I went on to develop a course on African American culture and communication which focused on African American cultural values and how they shaped communication practices. In addition, I collaborated with other faculty members at WCU in creating an African American Studies minor.

Equipped with this knowledge, I could reflect back on my up-bringing and those spaces which served as the homeplace—the first one being my childhood home in South Coatesville, Pennsylvania. I have fond memories of Sunday afternoons when my extended family would gather at our home. The house would be packed with my siblings, cousins, aunts, uncles and grandmother. Mom would prepare the Sunday meal of fried chicken, mashed potatoes, gravy, greens, rice, candied yams, tossed salad, rolls, and sometimes macaroni and cheese. There was always a Sunday dessert—homemade apple or cherry pie, or pineapple upside down cake, or my favorite, lemon meringue pie.

If it was football season, my dad would sometimes bring down a second TV from upstairs so we could watch two games in the living room. He would work the antennas on the smaller black and white TV to tune into WGAL 8 Lancaster to get the Steelers games. After the meal, the adults would have conversations which would always lead to some humorous comments or perspectives that would have people laughing, and laughing, and laughing. It wasn't a get-together in our family without laughter—often times something was said that would lead to crying laughing. If you weren't careful, your stomach and sides would be hurting later on from all the laughter. It was a community of African Americans where we talked, laughed, and broke bread together. Often, our friends would be at our house, too. To this day, I'm still in touch with my childhood friend, Cliff Robinson, who I have known since we were four or five years old. Cliff was like family. He and his younger sister would often be at our house (or I would be at his). At our small house, all were welcomed. Looking back it was the first community that bolstered me against the outside world—I came to understand I might be invisible and stereotyped in society, but in the home-place, we were the heroes of our own stories. We were just as good as anyone else.

Even now, although a good many of those relatives have passed on, when we get together as an extended family, it duplicates many of the cultural and communicative practices that I remember so well from when I was a little boy. They still re-energize and reaffirm my sense of self. There is comfort in the familiarity of those family practices that gives meaning and understanding to my identity. Those times together remind us we are human.

Over the years, I was fortunate enough to be part of other "homeplaces" that created and reaffirmed my sense of self—spaces where I was understood and humanized. As an undergraduate at WCU my friend group: Martin Wilson, Claude Taylor, Dave Lindenmuth, Daryl Flitcraft, and Terence Canady created an environment where we supported one another as we made our way through college to graduation. Our bond became very tight from those four years at WCU and we still remain friends. In addition to the faculty noted earlier who mentored me, my WCU friend group gave me the encouragement and the community to succeed. At each stop in my career, at Ohio University (such as the Miller's moments with J.W. Smith), at Buffalo State College, and then back to West Chester University, I was fortunate enough to have a homeplace.

As a faculty member at WCU, I thoroughly enjoyed the times I would gather with Skip Huston, Angie Howard, and Tammy James (collectively we had nearly 90 years of experience at WCU). I could go on and on about the times the Big Four got together for wings and conversation. It was a recurring moment of community—moments that reinforced our value and experiences as we navigated our careers in higher education.

Sometimes, however, life provides interesting twists in which the mascot is seen and heard. The spring of 2017 was one of those moments. It was late in the day, and I was in the department office. I looked up and standing in front of me was my old football coach from Coatesville Area Senior High School. I'll back up a minute and explain that this person wasn't the head coach when I was switched from QB to WR. This person came one year later—he was named head coach for my senior year. When he arrived, he changed the Coatesville system from a multiple-option attack to a more physical power running approach. All the hard work and familiarity of being in one system for my entire football career went by the wayside in the spring of 1986. This person brought a new system to Coatesville—a system that many did not fit. Instead of having a senior year in which we would finally arrive to finish our careers, it became an unsettling year attempting to learn a new system. Thus, senior year was a wash; I was "playing out the string." I started half a dozen games at free safety for a team that lacked an identity. We finished for the third straight season with a 5-7 record and a third straight loss to our arch rival, Downingtown High School, on Thanksgiving morning.

After that moment, I moved on from football, finished my senior year in the spring of 1987 and attended West Chester University as a Communication Studies major in the fall. My choice of major was influenced by a television class I took my junior and senior year at Coatesville Area Senior High School. For the class, I was a sports reporter for WCHS-TV which broadcast a daily announcement show in the high school and a weekly update show that aired on local cable TV.

In the years following my senior year, the new coach did have success with the football program. He eventually transitioned into administration and became the Coatesville Area School District Superintendent. When I returned to WCU as a faculty member (but before I became department chair) I ran into him on the WCU campus during a football game—I think there was a former Red Raider on the WCU roster. I gave him my card and told him to let me know if he ever wanted me to come back to talk to the students. I never heard from him.

Fast forward to the spring of 2017. This person standing in front of me had resigned amidst a scandal which revealed text exchanges with the athletic director laced with racial epithets demeaning African American and Latino staff and students. The board allowed him to resign without determining if any disciplinary action needed to be taken. However, the Chester County D.A. further investigated the incident. From the investigation, it was alleged he had illegally used school funds to purchase rings for the football team, and he was accused of nepotism. When he appeared in my office, he was awaiting his trial.

Former Coach: "Well, it looks like you have done well for yourself."

Me: "Yeah, things have been good."

Former Coach: "Now, don't you believe anything they say in the press . . ."

And before he could finish, I said, "I'm not here to judge. What brings you to campus?"

Former Coach: "I was participating in the DNA project, the professor said for me to stop down. I said, 'He doesn't want to see me.'"

Me: "Well, I'm glad you stopped down. And I'm glad you are participating in the DNA project—it's interesting hearing what people think about their ancestry before and after receiving their DNA results."

Former Coach: "I suppose so."

It was a strange and ironic moment hearing his southern drawl again—two people in two different places in their careers—passing one another in time. He entered my office with a perplexed look on his face, noting the various photos of me with well-known figures such as Michael Eric Dyson and Tamala Edwards. I guess he was making sense of things. I, on the other hand, hadn't thought about my senior year at Coatesville Area Senior High School in years, but it came back to me in one stunning moment. I was also making sense of things. He seemed tired, and his voice did not carry the same confidence and authority that I remembered from high school. He seemed resigned. We talked for about five minutes. We said our goodbyes. Then, as suddenly as he appeared, he disappeared. About a year later he was convicted of theft.[32]

As leaders, the most viable resource are the people around you. Too many leaders, however, fail to grasp this principle. Leaders can change and revitalize the organizational environment by seeing the uniqueness in each individual and determining how each person contributes to the mission of the organization. When leaders know and understand each individual in the unit, this moves people from the mascot to being human. It's a way for the leader to transform the organization from being a reflection of the outside world to creating a slice of the homeplace.

Chapter 7: We Need More Branch Rickeys

It was a short phone call but one with reverberating consequences. In the spring of 2017, I was informed another person was
selected for the position of Interim Dean of the College of Arts and
Humanities, but I was thanked for my willingness to serve and to
step up for the position. Sometimes the simplest statements have
the most dramatic effect in one's life. What became apparent to
me in that moment was my abilities and accomplishments, no matter how great, were not valued beyond the circles of individuals
who truly knew me. It was life imitating research. In 2006, I worked
with a colleague in the Psychology Department completing an ex-
tensive research project that analyzed mentoring in organizations
including higher education. The research led to the creation of the
faculty mentoring program at WCU. In our research, one theme we
identified from the literature was that people of color have fewer

connections to professional and social networks within organizations—thus, limiting their ability to rise in organizations.

In addition to being familiar with the research about the need for minority faculty mentoring, I had researched and written extensively about African American males, especially African American athletes. In my article on Donovan McNabb, I illustrated how every major African American athlete in Philly (including Wilt Chamberlain), despite success, was eventually pushed out of town.[33] These two research findings were my reality in the spring of 2017. It was clear I had gone as high as I could—it was time to look outward instead of inward for the next opportunity.

That brief phone conversation was 1985 all over again—when I was denied the opportunity to play quarterback. At that moment in 1985, I stopped drinking the red and black Kool Aid of Coatesville Area Senior High School. Likewise in 2017, I stopped drinking the purple and gold Kool Aid of WCU.

"What's next?" was the question. After reflecting upon my career, I inquired into different ways I could serve or assist the university. I submitted a proposal to assist with advising African American and Latino male students in the effort to improve their graduation and retention rates. I even conducted focus groups with African American/Latino male students in the fall of 2017 to generate ideas for their success. Nothing came of the offer.

In 1960, upon returning home to Louisville, Kentucky with an Olympic Gold Medal in boxing, Muhammad Ali (then Cassius Clay) was refused service at a local restaurant. Ali who was publicly referred to as the "Olympic nigger" walked to the Second Street Bridge and tossed his medal into the Ohio River to protest his second class citizenship in the United States.[34] In 2017, symbolically, I threw out all my mementos.

After 16 years—I was still the mascot. The organization didn't know me and more importantly didn't value me or my work. It's strange when you think you're on the team, but then realize you never were. Malcolm X's words rang true, "I was *with* them but not considered *of* them."

In my own way, I voiced my dissatisfaction by putting LeBron James' statement on my office door—his statement was in response to the n-word being spray painted on his home in LA:

> "No matter how much money you have, no matter how famous you are, no matter how many people admire you, being black in America is—it's tough," James said. "And we got a long way to go for us as a society and for us as African-Americans until we feel equal in America."[35]

It was a straight-forward comment that not only captured the state of being black in America but my situation as well.

Many leaders will have moments when they feel stuck. They lose an election, they decide to step down for family or health reasons. They get burned out. Sometimes there is no clear direction when leaving one position to determine the next. When you look across higher education and many industries in general—there is a lack of African American men in leadership positions. [36] If true transformation is to occur in organizations, it must be initiated by individuals in power who have vision and commitment to real diversity. They must be people who are authentic, who value diversity, who support people and know how to build teams and not cliques. Denny Klinzing had done that for me. Interestingly, if it wasn't for Denny, I would not have made it back to WCU. What is needed in higher education is more Branch Rickeys and fewer Bull Connors.

Branch Rickey was the owner of the Brooklyn Dodgers during the time major league baseball was still segregated. Rickey was a man ahead of his time as he knew segregation in baseball needed to end. To break the color line, Rickey was committed to finding the ideal African American because that person would pave the way for others.

My intention is not to recount how Rickey selected Jackie Robinson and the racism that Robinson had to endure as the first African American major league player. Rather, the point I'm making is that Rickey valued and believed in Jackie Robinson. He was committed to Robinson's success. Everyone needs a supporter to get him or her to the next level. In 2017, there were no Branch Rickeys on my campus. Interestingly, when I was applying for other positions and having a one-on-one conversation about the process with a high ranking organizational member, the person stated, "You're an African American male in higher education; you're highly desirable." Funny how my "desirability" was for other institutions but not for my own campus.

As leaders, our job is to support and pour into others so they can reach their destiny. We have to recognize the leadership potential in those with whom we work. What are the person's goals? What is the person good at and what are the person's strengths? What experiences does the person possess that enrich the organization? How can the person best use his or her talents and abilities?

Effective leaders have to constantly, introspectively assess the people around them and assist in their personal and professional development. Too many times it's the opposite. From my time as a department chair, I observed leaders dictating without direction, treating people like things, and failing to motivate or support others. Instead of building upon a person's experience, the leaders who I observed when I was a department chair undervalued people who worked for them. From my experience, few leaders invested the time or had the patience to teach others how to be successful.

In contrast, over the years, I developed a leadership style that was based upon what I learned through sports. From my perspective exceptional leaders are effective coaches who are outstanding teachers. In the world of sports, coaching provides a slew of examples of individuals who can take players who might be average and elevate them to greatness because the coach knows how to teach, instruct, and motivate.

Successful coaches adapt game plans to their players, teach them how to get better, and motivate them in order to maximize their performance. For example, I'm not a Patriots fan, but you have to give credit where credit is due. Bill Bellicheck might be one of the best coaches of all time because he is able to get the most out of his players, and he has done it over a long period of time—many times without the best players—oftentimes with cast offs from other teams. However, the Patriots are in contention year after year. In an era of free agency, it is unheard of to maintain the level of success the Patriots have had.

Furthermore, I firmly believe individuals can be effective leaders if they are given the opportunity and support. My belief was reaffirmed through the great example of the Philadelphia Eagles Super Bowl season of 2017-18. In short, the Eagles had not won a world title since 1960. Eagles fans endured many heartbreaks and set-backs during the championship drought. Some Eagle fans even wondered if they would ever see an Eagles championship in their lifetime.

Enter new Eagles head coach Doug Peterson, in 2016. He replaced Chip Kelly the highly decorated college coach who was ineffective as an NFL coach. When Peterson was hired, he was not a popular choice. Some "experts" indicated that Peterson was the worst hire by an NFL team that year.[37] Peterson did not have a lot of accolades. He was a journeymen NFL QB, mostly in backup roles. He moved up in coaching responsibilities for Andy Reid at Kansas City, eventually becoming the offensive coordinator, but he didn't call plays. On the surface, he looked like a safe hire but not a championship caliber one. To complicate the situation, going into his second year his team had a rash of season-ending injuries, the most problematic being his second year QB, Carson Wentz, who was having a MVP season until his ACL injury.

However, what many overlooked was Peterson's ability to connect with players and his ability to adapt to his players. What might be his greatest attribute is how he believes in his players which helped him immensely when the team had to replace injured players with back-up players. When Peterson had to go with back-up QB Nick Foles after week 14, no one expected the Eagles to win the Super Bowl. What Peterson did, however, was adapt to his players. When he had to put Foles into the starting line-up, Peterson did not expect Foles to be Carson Wentz and run the same plays as Wentz.

Foles and Wentz are two different players with different strengths. How many coaches or leaders, however, would have expected Foles to perform just like Wentz and would not have adjusted the game plan for Foles?

To Peterson's credit, he did not force his system onto Foles. Rather, Peterson did the opposite, adjusting his system to fit Foles' skills and abilities. He watched old game films when Foles was a starter earlier in his career to identify what he did well. Peterson reviewed the films with Foles, discussed with him what plays he was most comfortable with, and adapted plays to fit Foles' skill set. As you can imagine, determining how to adapt the offense to Foles' skill set (especially after 14 weeks in a 17-week season), was extra work for Peterson. However, as the leader, he wanted to put Foles in the best possible position to help the team win.

The result: Despite being underdogs in each playoff game and the Super Bowl, the Eagles won each playoff game and defeated one of the most successful franchises of all time, the New England Patriots in the Super Bowl. Foles led the Eagles to their first Super Bowl victory and was named MVP of the Super Bowl. Who would have thought that an untested coach and a back-up QB would out duel arguably the best head coach/QB combination of all time, Belichick and Brady? One of the best moments from the Super Bowl came when the Eagles faced a fourth down and goal. Instead of being conservative and kicking a field goal, Peterson went for it with their "Philly Special" play in which Foles caught the TD pass. After the Super Bowl, footage surfaced of the dialogue that took place as Foles and Peterson strategized on what play to run. During their sideline discussion, the footage showed Foles asking Peterson to run the "Philly Special" (not the coach dictating to the player). Peterson agreed and never wavered. It was the ultimate example of believing in people and adapting to an individual's skill set. In the process, the Eagles succeeded.

What Peterson accomplished was amazing. Very few coaches would have been able to manage the number of injuries and be willing to adapt the team's style of play for back-up players to be successful. Too many coaches (and leaders), force a system onto individuals without accounting for what these individuals can and cannot achieve. There is a famous saying about leadership as it relates to Dean Smith when he was Michael Jordan's college coach at the University of North Carolina. Jordan, who would later become one of the greatest NBA players of all-time, did not show his explosiveness as an offensive player at UNC due to Dean Smith's offensive system. The joke was: "The only man to stop Michael Jordan was Dean Smith."

If Peterson would have expected Foles to perform like Wentz, I'm not sure the Eagles would have won the Super Bowl. Rather than asking Foles to attempt plays he couldn't execute, Peterson focused on what Foles could do. As a result, Foles, the players, and the team succeeded. The same is true with leaders—if leaders expect all employees to conform to one system and assume all employees have the same abilities, the leader will not get the most out of his or her employees. Effective leaders don't change their organizational goals or standards; instead they are flexible about how different employees can accomplish these goals. The key is allowing employees to use their strengths instead of taking a "one size fits all" approach to achieving goals.

In addition to adaptive leadership, Peterson's example demonstrates that a person who is given a chance and who is supported can be successful. There is no doubt any individual can be a leader—the person just needs the opportunity and support.[38]

Looking back on my days as a department chair, one of the aspects I took the most pride in was assisting in students' success. I have given opportunities and support to many students and faculty along the way to assist them in accomplishing their goals—whether it was landing their first job, preparing students from our graduate program for acceptance into Ph.D. programs, supporting adjunct professors and helping some transition into permanent teaching positions, shepherding colleagues within and outside the department through tenure and promotion, helping students who were facing academic challenges (even expulsion), and getting them past the challenges to graduation. The list goes on and on of how I helped unlock others' potential as others in the past unlocked my potential.

Leaders greatly impact their organizations by who they elevate into leadership positions, who they select for opportunities, and what ideas they support. What leaders are committed to can create positive change and unleash the potential in others. Leaders like Branch Rickey and Doug Peterson created positive change by valuing the uniqueness in individuals and adapting to individual strengths. There were a lot of talented African American baseball players in the 1940s, but Rickey needed the right individual who could perform on the field yet be tough enough to endure racism on and off the field. Peterson when confronted with playing his back-up quarterback didn't expect Foles to be Carson Wentz. Instead, he tailored the offense to Foles' strengths in order for him to succeed. Effective leaders look for the leadership potential in others, and they adapt and assist others to help them be successful. If anyone has any doubt what effective leadership looks like, just review the season of the 2017-18 Philadelphia Eagles.

Chapter 8: All Aboard the Mothership!

"A true leader has the confidence to stand alone, the courage to make tough decisions, and the compassion to listen to the needs of others."

– Douglas McArthur

In the summer of 2017, I had the opportunity to visit the National Museum of African American History and Culture on the national mall in Washington, D.C. The vast collection of documents and artifacts which tell the African American experience are moving, enlightening, and inspiring. The exhibits that capture African Americans' contribution to culture and society provide an uplifting narrative of what was, is, and can be.[39] On the "Cultural Expressions" floor, many artifacts depict the contributions of African Americans to music. One item, Parliament's Mothership, is displayed on this floor. Associated with George Clinton and the Parliament-Funkadelic performers, the Mothership, was a metallic, 1500-pound, triangular spaceship made of metal, plastic, and glass.

In the history of music, the Mothership represented one of the most iconic stage props ever used in concerts. As a memorable closing to their concerts, the funk band lowered the Mothership to the stage to symbolically represent "funk deliverance." When concert goers reached "funk deliverance," everyone was symbolically emancipated and transported to a place free of racism and oppression. P-Funk closed their concerts by symbolically liberating African Americans and reminding America of its founding ideals.

Similar to how the Mothership transported individuals from an oppressive reality to an ideal state, effective leadership is about transforming a lackluster organizational climate into a dynamic and empowering environment. Boarding the Mothership means leaving an imperfect state for an improved one based upon mutual respect and understanding. On the Mothership, we enjoy the ride and the destination. Effective leaders build relationships with and among the passengers while creating a vision for the voyage to provide meaning for the journey and the destination.

Effective leaders seek ways to increase opportunities for others to board the Mothership. As an example, when LeBron James opened the I Promise School, a school for at-risk kids in Akron, Ohio, in 2018 he stated:

I want people to know that these kids should still have the same opportunity as everybody else. That's what's most important. Us as adults, we have a responsibility to not let these kids down, to continue to be the teachers, the mentors, the parents, the coaching, the life skills, the superheroes . . . whatever it is that gives the inspiration, everything, that's our responsibility. These kids are our future and they have dreams and aspirations bigger than the city of Akron, than the state of Ohio, than the USA.[40]

Although James is talking about the I Promise School, the principles he articulates reinforce the importance of providing opportunities for people so they can be successful. That is leadership! James is expanding the Mothership.

At this point in my career, I can look back at those individuals who encouraged me and built authentic relationships that assisted me in my growth and development as a faculty member and leader. I can also look back and identify the students, faculty members, and individuals who I have assisted in their growth and development. It's my small way of increasing the number of people who can board the Mothership. I was reminded of this fact when I was honored by the Eastern Communication Association (ECA) in the spring of 2019 as a Distinguished Teaching Fellow and as a Distinguished Research Fellow. Both awards are very selective as only one percent of the membership in any given year can receive this award—the teaching award recognizes a distinguished career of teaching excellence while the research award recognizes distinguished research in the field of communication. Both awards highlight teacher-scholars who have at least ten years of active membership and continuous service to ECA.

I was humbled and honored to be nominated by my colleagues in the field and to receive these awards—awards I could not even imagine as a young boy from Coatesville who struggled with writing. It was very rewarding to receive the nomination letters from former students, faculty, and colleagues expressing the positive impact I had on them as a teacher and as a scholar. Many of the comments from my former students and colleagues articulated themes of my leadership philosophy of providing opportunities and support. I have included two of these nomination letters below:

It is with great pleasure I write a letter of support for Dr. Tim Brown for the teaching fellows honor. I owe Dr. Brown a great deal of gratitude for playing a pivotal role in helping me obtain the academic position I currently hold. Now I see him as a dear friend, but for more than a decade, well after grad school, he has been an exceptional mentor to me. He truly represents the best of what our field has to offer as a teacher and as a colleague.

When I came to West Chester University for my undergraduate degree, Dr. Brown was the chair of the Communication Studies Department. I was a Com Studies major but went through a period where my grades were very poor, and I was considering alternate options for my degree and career. During this time, Dr. Brown served as a primary source of guidance. He always made time for me when I wanted to discuss my future. Over many instances, he helped me move closer to where I am today. Whether it was giving me a chance to be a part of the master's program, writing letters of recommendation, sharing adjunct opportunities, talking about life, or showing me around ECA, Dr. Brown acted altruistically at all times. I didn't benefit him; he just helped me because he is genuinely unselfish and cares for others. His advice and guidance led me to get my doctorate in Communications and a full-time faculty position at xxx, which I currently hold.

Aside from his character as a mentor and advisor, Dr. Brown was also one of my favorite teachers of all time. In my masters, he taught a course on critical/cultural studies. He opened my eyes to the many ways that rhetoric can be used to oppress groups of people and re-inforce power. To this day, I use some of the lessons and articles that he discussed in that class. Next week I am presenting a lesson on hegemony, and most of it came from what Dr. Brown taught me. I also learned a great deal about pedagogy from Dr. Brown, simply by analyzing his teaching style. The way he taught class made con-tent very real. He had an uncanny ability to take readings and make them palpable for the class. Learning rhetorical criticism can be particularly difficult because the language and frameworks used by authors can be intricate and hard to understand. Yet, through his teaching style, Dr. Brown made every article relatable and easy to comprehend. He turned the language of academics into language a novice learner could understand without taking away from the significance of the original conceptualization. As a student in his class, you never felt as though you were being spoke down to. Rather, you were a part of his team, working towards learning outcomes. This is no small task, but Dr. Brown was truly a master at it.

The most important lesson Dr. Brown taught me, though, was how to interact with students. There was no reason for him to give me a second chance as an undergraduate student with poor grades and an undecided attitude about the field of communication. There was no reason for him to be such a sincere individual and give me so much of his office time just to talk about what I wanted to do with my life. There is no reason for him to still check up on me today just to make sure all is well in my career and see if I will be at ECA. What I learned the most from him is to be conscious of my communication. His ability to be understanding, kind, and genuine towards students is what Dr. Brown is known for. He always has the time to greet you with a smile and listen to what you have to say, regardless of who you are. The way I carry myself as a professor is largely emulated from what I learned from interacting with Dr. Brown.

In conclusion, Dr. Tim Brown is an excellent professor and although your award may not reciprocate all the amazing work he has done over the years, it will certainly acknowledge his excellence as a teacher, colleague, and administrator along with the fact that he has substantially changed many lives for the better for well over a decade. He is an exceptional individual, someone that I greatly respect, and someone that I firmly believe is the most deserving of being honored at ECA. Thank you for reading my words and if you have any further questions feel free to contact me directly!

• • •

I hope this letter finds you well. I am writing on behalf of Dr. Timothy Brown, who I understand has been nominated for the Eastern Communication Association's Teaching Fellows honor, a nomination I know he very much deserves. I would like to recommend Dr. Brown on the basis of his teaching style, his rapport with students, and his approach to assignments and class time, all of which had a strong impact on my experience as a student at West Chester University.

I met Dr. Brown during a leadership communication course at West Chester during my first semester as a graduate student. He was the friendly face who welcomed us all in with a smile and his trademark warm personality. He had high expectations for us as students, and though the standards were formidable, we always wanted to raise the bar because impressing Dr. Brown was such a valuable accomplishment.

Beyond challenging us in the classroom, Dr. Brown always looked for enrichment opportunities for his students. He helped me prepare my papers for conferences such as ECA or NCA, and then introduced me to colleagues and helped me network at conferences. For ECA in Providence, Rhode Island a few years ago, he rented a van and woke up at 4:00 a.m. to pick us up and drive us all the way from West Chester to Providence for the conference.

As my independent study advisor, he was always happy to advise me on my career and scholarship journey. His mentorship is one of the reasons I decided to pursue a Ph.D. His encouragement has meant everything. For these reasons, I am honored to provide my wholehearted recommendation on Dr. Brown's behalf for the ECA Teaching Fellow honor. Please let me know if you have any questions or would like more information.

Comments like these reaffirm why I chose a career in higher education. As Denny told me years ago—institutions exist to change students' lives. I'm glad to have had a small part in the success of my students and my colleagues. The ideas expressed here demonstrate what I have learned, how I have been helped, and how I have embraced a service-leadership approach in higher education. With the right leadership, we can all board the Mothership.

Despite how rewarding it is to be a leader and the number of people you help along the way, my story is an example for leaders to not be naïve about how others will perceive you. *No One Cheers for Goliath* because Goliath is supposed to win. The physical and mental abilities that define Goliath's prowess also become the target of detractors, detractors who are cantankerous when something goes wrong, but are silent when everything is going well. For Chamberlain, his critics measured his career by improbable standards of perfection, instead of appreciating him for his uniqueness. What he didn't accomplishment somehow overshadowed what he did accomplish—which is staggering given that he holds over 70 NBA records—many that will never be broken!

What applies to Chamberlain, applies to leadership. No matter how many accomplishments and accolades, no matter how effective the leader is in leading a group, individuals in your own organization will take your leadership for granted. That is the paradox of leadership—to be effective is to be underappreciated. The more you accomplish the less it will be recognized. Leadership is like Sisyphus pushing the rock up the hill only to have it roll back down.

Despite the challenges of being a leader, from difficult colleagues to decision making to work/life balance, being a leader does offer a sense of reward and accomplishment when the effort is focused on helping others. In my years as a department chair, the ideas and principles I have discussed in this book can be summarized in the following principles.

Effective leadership is an attitude!

The attitude of the leader is what drives the culture of the organization. At the heart of an organization's culture are authentic and genuine relationships. Positive work environments don't happen by themselves, they must be developed. You are who you attract. If the leader is not invested, lacks emotional intelligence, or dislikes working with people, the organization will not achieve at a high level no matter how talented the people are. Creating a positive work environment is up to the leader. It's like being a farmer. If you don't cultivate the ground, you won't yield the best crops. The same is true in work environments.

Lead people, manage things.

In leadership, people are your greatest asset. If the leader cultivates a positive work environment where individuals feel valued and supported, then they can achieve almost anything. And when people are doing their best work, the organization can function and achieve at a high level. Too many leaders get caught up in a "one size fits all" leadership style that undermines creativity and innovation. A rule, bylaw, or reified practice never motivated or inspired anyone to achieve a near unattainable goal. Leaders must know their co-workers in order to put them in the best possible position to be successful. When people achieve, the organization benefits.

If there is no struggle, there is no progress.

In leadership, there will be struggle, but struggle leads to progress. Leading people towards organizational goals is not easy. There will be challenges; there will be set-backs; there will be mistakes. Effective leaders have experienced the struggle and have learned how to stay focused to navigate the challenges. Leaders must be mindful that employees have struggles too; emotional intelligence is key to helping them through these struggles even ones that remain unnamed. Effective leadership identifies and provides opportunities and support to enable others to succeed.

You can't make people "do right."

People will test you. People will act in their own self-interest. People will look for loopholes. People will let you down. As leaders, we can lead the way; we can tell people what we expect, but we can't control how others act. We can only control how we react. This is an important lesson of leadership. As a leader, you can set the example, you can be a servant-leader, you can set the tone for how to complete tasks, show people how to sacrifice, and how to treat one another, but at the end of the day the other people you lead must catch the vision. Leaders can't make people do the right thing, we can only lead the way.

"All my skinfolk, ain't kinfolk"

Don't assume if you share similarities with a person that these similarities translate to support. Leaders have to be keen discerners of people, their motives, and their character. Thus, three principles are apparent: 1) Any leader is a target, 2) Don't underestimate the lengths someone will go to get their own way, 3) Don't be surprised if the person targeting you is one of your own kind. Leaders must be on guard at all times. Know what your supporters are doing but also know what your detractors are doing. Knowing what the opposition is doing keeps you informed and can prevent you from being blindsided.

Mascot: Going beyond superficial relationships

Regardless of a person's background, training, and life experience, at times, there will be doubt whether you are being selected for your skills and abilities or if you are being selected for appearances. The interactions we have, the topics we discuss, who is included (and excluded) during formal meetings or informal gatherings all reveal who is and isn't part of the club. If organizations are going to optimize their opportunities, the leader must build authentic relationships to unlock the potential in others. Seeing humanity in everyone and relating to everyone as human beings goes a long way in bolstering the self-value and self-respect of individuals in the organization. Leaders greatly impact their organizations by who they elevate into leadership positions, who they select for opportunities, and what ideas they support. What leaders commit themselves to can create positive change (reveal his or her values) and can unleash the potential in others.

We need more Branch Rickeys.

To be effective, a leader must value the uniqueness of individuals and must adapt to individual strengths to create positive change. There is an old saying, "You don't go to war with the army you wish you had, you go to war with the army you do have." Effective leaders must elevate the performance of the people around them by knowing their abilities and skills and maximizing those abilities and skills. A leader can't expect a person to run like Usain Bolt, but the leader can maximize the person's running ability to get the most out of their performance. Leaders such as Branch Rickey and Doug Peterson created positive change by valuing the uniqueness of individuals, giving them an opportunity, and adapting to their strengths. As a result, the organizations they led accomplished great things.

Equipped with these ideas, a leader can be effective. While these ideas still might not result in people cheering for Goliath, they will reassure any leader who is trying to lead in an ethical and empowering way. As you work with and support those around you, they will be able to reach their goals. When they reach their goals, this enables the organization to achieve its goals. And in the process, we are all able to enjoy the ride aboard the Mothership as well as the destination.

Epilogue

Jesus looked at them and said, "With man this is impossible,
but with God all things are possible."
- *Matthew 19:26 New International Version (NIV)*

When you are willing to focus on getting the job done as opposed to being concerned about who gets the credit, you will be more successful and you will achieve goals in an authentic and ethical manner. Each endeavor you undertake has the potential to lead to your next opportunity. That was true for me. My internship experience led to the opportunity to be recruited back to West Chester University as a Graduate Assistant for the Forensics Team in the Communication Studies graduate program. Working as a Graduate Assistant for the Forensics Team led to the opportunity to work as a Graduate Assistant with the Forensics Team as a doctoral student at Ohio University where I met my wife. At Ohio University, I was given support to present my research at the National Communication Association, which led to meeting faculty from Buffalo State College which led to my first faculty position. I can go on and on. Anything is possible when you work unto the Lord.

What God has made possible in my academic journey no one could have predicted or foreseen. No matter what position I held in higher education, I worked unto the Lord using those leadership principles I learned while organizing the neighborhood kids for our athletic games in Green Field. In each endeavor, I have been fortunate to be supported by individuals who believed in me and gave me the support I needed to lead faculty, staff, and students. In turn, I have tried to emulate these leadership lessons by providing others with opportunities and support.

In any journey, there will be times when it is unclear what the next leadership opportunity will be when a current leadership position ends. That was my situation in December of 2016. I had to have faith I would have an opportunity to demonstrate my skills and abilities at another institution in another system. In my post-chair year, I returned to the faculty taking on a full teaching schedule. In some ways it was liberating as instead of managing and shepherding an entire department, I could focus on my classes, my students, and my research. Even though as a department chair I still taught every summer, going back to full-time teaching and teaching well reaffirmed that I still "had it" as a teacher.

During my post-chair year, when I ran into colleagues who I knew from other institutions at conferences they would ask me, "What's next?" or "You should be a dean." At one point, I had a brief conversation with one of my former professors from Ohio University. He was a prominent teacher-scholar in the discipline who had served as President of our National Communication Association. He said to me, "Tim, you should be a dean. You have all the skills and abilities to be one, and we need people like you in one of those positions. You can't sit on all your years of experience as department chair." I really appreciated the vote of confidence from such a prominent person in the field. It was the nudge I needed to seriously pursue dean positions.

In the spring of 2018, I was the guest speaker for our Lambda Pi Eta induction ceremony. I enjoyed giving a yearly motivational speech as part of their induction ceremony. Growing up, I was a huge fan of the Peanuts (Charlie Brown) TV specials. Typically, I would work in a theme from one of the specials as a way to incorporate humor and a life lesson for the students since Charlie Brown always had to deal with disappointment in life from his friends, from his family, even from his dog Snoopy. In this particular speech, I highlighted something different from the series—taking risks. I framed for the audience how sometimes taking risks is necessary to achieve a goal. I discussed this point within the context of how Lucy would always hold a football for Charlie Brown to kick but never let him kick it. Charlie Brown would try, but each time at the very last moment, Lucy would pull the ball away. No matter how much Charlie Brown planned, schemed, or ran, he was never allowed to kick the ball. I explained how Charlie Brown not being allowed to kick the ball was a metaphor for life. No matter how prepared you are or what skills you possess, if people are preventing you from ascending you will not reach your goal. In the speech, I said:

We should commend Charlie Brown for not giving up in his quest to kick the ball. He showed determination and a great deal of commitment. However, over the years, I have developed a new interpretation of him not being allowed to kick the ball. If they aren't allowing you to kick the ball, go find another ball to kick!

Emphasizing "go find another ball to kick," to the audience was liberating. Not many knew it, but I was not only motivating the students, I was also motivating myself. It was time for me to find "another ball to kick." I was ready for the change.

Change can bring about rebirth and a renewed spirit fueled by a new opportunity and a new call. In May of 2018, I received that opportunity. After completing two and a half days of on-campus interviews, I was offered the position of Dean of the James L. Knight

School of Communication at Queens University of Charlotte—the only School of Communication in the nation endowed by the Knight Foundation. My improbable journey, as a first-generation college student, would continue in the New South.

The moment was a little overwhelming. After all these years, I still saw myself as that young boy who organized games for the neighborhood kids at Green Field on Remington Avenue in South Coatesville. Self-conscious but organized, amiable but driven, consistent but not flashy, and more introvert than extrovert, I was able to develop and build upon these traits as a leader of people due to the assistance of mentors and life experiences.

By accepting the position of Dean of the Knight School of Communication at Queens University of Charlotte, I would continue to grow and develop as a leader. As daunting as this transformation seemed, I needed to try. I needed to try not only for myself but for all those young boys and girls who might only have nothing else but a dream. If there is anything that can be learned from my story—it does not matter where you start or what you have (or don't have)—with self-confidence and a network of opportunity and support, you can succeed. As Robert Kennedy once said, "Some men see things as they are, and ask why. I dream of things that never were and ask why not."

Being yourself matters. Treating people as human and building authentic relationships matters. Having a sense of humor matters.

Working toward the greater good matters. Striving to lead for the greater good matters. Working to expand opportunity and social mobility for others matters. It is these principles that I have been led by and by which I lead others. Providing opportunity and giving support are a true indication of effective leadership.

Notes

[1] "Legend's Profile: Wilt Chamberlain," accessed February 7, 2020, https://www.nba.com/history/legends/profiles/wilt-chamberlain

[2] Quoted in Frank Litsky, "Wilt Chamberlain, Who Dominated Basketball for 14 Seasons, Is Dead at 63," *The New York Times*, October 12, 1999, https://archive.nytimes.com/www.nytimes.com/library/sports/basketball/101399bkn-obit-chamberlain.html

[3] "Wilt Chamberlain's NBA Records," NBA.com, accessed January 25, 2018. http://archive.nba.com/encyclopedia/wilts_records.html

[4] Quoted in "The Day Wilt Chamberlain, NBA Legend, Died at 63 in 1999," *New York Daily News*, last modified October 12, https://www.nydailynews.com/sports/basketball/nba-legend-wilt-chamberlain-dies-1999-article-1.2393843.
[5] "The Day Wilt Chamberlain;" Litsky, "Wilt Chamberlain."

[6] Avi Wolfman-Arvent, "Pa. provides some of the worst opportunities for students of color, reports say," *The Philadelphia Tribune*, January 15, 2020, https://www.phillytrib.com/news/state_and_region/pa-provides-some-of-the-worst-opportunities-for-students-of/article_611dddb6-380a-11ea-b6cd-f33353028ce8.html; Caroline Helms, "PA Ranked 47th Worst State for Opportunities for Students of Color," *The Quad*. February 3, 2020, 1-2.

[7] "WTC Steel Beams Return to Penn. Home for Museum Display," NBC New York, last modified April 14, 2010, https://www.nbcnewyork.com/news/local/wtc-steel-beams-return-to-penn-home-for-museum-display/1910516/

[8] "Celebs who went from failures to success stories," CBS News, Accessed August 12, 2018. https://www.cbsnews.com/pictures/celebs-who-went-from-failures-to-success-stories/8/

[9] Due to the population growth in the Downingtown Area School District, Downingtown High School split into two high schools in 2003, Downingtown West High School (the Whippets) and Downingtown East High School (the Cougars), while Coatesville has remained as one high school.

[10] See Appendix A for one of the field hockey articles I wrote for the *Coatesville Record* (fall 1991).

[11] *Celtics/Lakers: Best of Enemies*. Directed by Jim Podhoretz. ESPN Films: 30 for 30, 2017.

[12] Frederick Douglass, *Narrative of the Life of Frederick Douglass: An American Slave* (Boston: The Anti-Slavery Office, 1845; New York: Laurel, 1997), 1. Citations refer to the Laurel edition.

[13] Frederick Douglas Institute https://www.wcupa.edu/_academics/fdouglass/

[14] Frederick Douglass, "West India Emancipation," speech delivered at Canandaigua, New York, August 3, 1857. In *Frederick Douglass: Selected Speeches and Writings*, Philip S. Foner, ed, Chicago, Lawrence Hill Books 1999, 367.

[15] See Brown, Timothy J. "Public Memory as Contested Site: The Struggle for Existence at the National Museum of African American History and Culture." In *U.S. Public Memory, Rhetoric, and the National Mall,* edited by Roger Aden, 163-164. New York: Lexington Books, 2018; Brown, Timothy J. "Scripting the Black Male Athlete: Donovan McNabb and the Double Bind of Black Masculinity." In *Masculinity in the Black Imagination: Politics of Communicating Race and Manhood,* edited by Ronald L. Jackson and Mark Hopson, 147-168. New York: Peter Lang Publishers, 2011.

[16] "Rebecca Lukens Resource Center," The National Iron & Steel Heritage Museum, accessed February 14, 2020, https://www.steelmuseum.org/RebeccaLukens/rebecca_lukens_resource_center/index.cfm

[17] "Coatesville, PA," Data USA, accessed February 14, 2020, https://datausa.io/profile/geo/coatesville-pa/

[18] "Chester County, PA" Data USA, accessed February 14, 2020, https://datausa.io/profile/geo/chester-county-pa#demographics; "Coatesville, PA," Data USA, accessed February 14, 2020, https://datausa.io/profile/geo/coatesville-pa/

[19] The "Coatesville Address" given by John Jay Chapman which chronicled the barbarity of the lynching is covered well in: Edwin Black, *Rhetorical Criticism: A Study in Method* (New York: The Macmillan Company, 1965) 78-90.

[20] Brown, "Public Memory," 163.
[21] Jonathan Lai and Erin McCarthy, "Coatesville Students Walk Out in Protest Over Racist Pumpkin Carvings," *The Philadelphia Inquirer*, October 20, 2017,

https://www.inquirer.com/philly/education/coatesville-high-school-protest-racism-carved-pumpkins-20171020.html

[22] See Appendix B for a copy of President Carter's letter.

[23] *Dawn of the Planet of the Apes*. Directed by Matt Reeves. Los Angeles: 20th Century Fox, 2014.

[24] Bryan DeArdo, "Terry Bradshaw Says He Will Never Talk About Chuck Noll Again," CBSSports.com, November 25, 2016, https://www.cbssports.com/nfl/news/terry-bradshaw-says-he-will-never-talk-about-chuck-noll-again/

[25] T.D. Jakes, "Three Types of People." Accessed August 16, 2018. https://youtu.be/W8NLOKlOc1I.

[26] Malcolm X, *The Autobiography of Malcolm X* (New York: Grove Press, 1965: New York: Ballantine Books, 1999), 28. Citations refer to the Ballantine edition.

[27] Jabari Mahiri, "Buffalo scholar: Fights for equity in the academy," in *African American Males in Higher Education Leadership*, ed. Patricia A. Mitchell (New York: Peter Lang, 2017), 1-14; George Yancy, "The Ugly Truth of Being a Black Professor in America." *The Chronicle of Higher Education*, April 29, 2018, https://www.chronicle.com/article/The-Ugly-Truth-of-Being-a/243234

[28] bell hooks, *Yearning: Race, Gender, and Cultural Practice* (Boston: South End Press, 1990), 41-50.

[29] John R. Rickford and Russell J. Rickford, *Spoken Soul: The Story of Black English* (New York: John Wiley & Sons) 2000, ix.

[30] Timothy J. Brown, "Allen Iverson as America's Most Wanted: Black Masculinity as a Cultural Site of Struggle," *Journal of Intercultural Communication Research* 34, no. 2 (2005): 65-87; Timothy J. Brown, "Scripting the Black Male Athlete: Donovan McNabb and the Double Bind of Black Masculinity" in *Masculinity in the Black Imagination: Politics of Communicating Race and Manhood,* eds. Ronald L. Jackson and Mark Hopson (New York: Peter Lang, 2011), 147-168; Sean Fourney and Timothy J. Brown, "More Than a Game: Fulfilling Expectations and Inscriptions in the Career of LeBron James," *The Western Journal of Black Studies,* 42, no. 3-4 (2018): 97-112.

[31] Timothy J. Brown, "Reaffirming African American Cultural Values: Tupac Shakur's Greatest Hits as a Musical Autobiography," *The Western Journal of Black Studies,* 29, no. 1 (2005): 558-573; Timothy J. Brown, "'I am who I am':

Black Masculinity and the Interpretation of Individualism in the Film *Barbershop*," *Qualitative Research Reports in Communication,* 9 no. 1 (2008): 46-61.

[32] Michael Rellahan, "Ex-Coatesville School Boss Guilty," *Daily Local News*, January 26, 2018. Accessed August 21, 2018, http://www.dailylocal.com/general-news/20180126/ex-coatesville-school-boss-guilty

[33] Timothy J. Brown, "Scripting the Black Male Athlete: Donovan McNabb and the Double Bind of Black Masculinity" in *Masculinity in the Black Imagination: Politics of Communicating Race and Manhood,* eds. Ronald L. Jackson and Mark Hopson (New York: Peter Lang, 2011), 147-168.

[34] Anthony O. Edmonds, *Muhammad Ali: A Biography.* (Westport: Greenwood Press, 2006), 40; Thomas R. Hietala, "Muhammad Ali and the Age of Bare-Knuckle Politics," *Muhammad Ali, The People's Champ,* ed. Elliott J. Gorn (Urbana: University of Illinois Press, 1995), 120-121.

[35] Scott Cacciola and Jonah E. Bromwich, "LeBron James Responds to Racial Vandalism: 'Being Black in America is Tough,' *The New York Times*, May 31, 2017, https://www.nytimes.com/2017/05/31/sports/lebron-racist-graffiti-home.html

[36] Emma Whitford, "There are so few that have made their way." Insidehighered.com, October 28, 2020, https://www.insidehighered.com/news/2020/10/28/black-administrators-are-too-rare-top-ranks-higher-education-it%E2%80%99s-not-just-pipeline

[37] Rob Tornoe, "ESPN Ranks Doug Peterson as NFL's Worst Coaching Hire," *Philly.com*, January 18, 2016, http://www.philly.com/philly/blogs/pattisonave/ESPN-ranks-Doug-Pederson-as-NFLs-worst-coaching-hire.html?arc404=true

[38] While Peterson's run as Philly's head coach ended abruptly after the 2020-21 season (despite having a winning record in the regular season and playoffs), his leadership during the Eagles' first Super Bowl season still deserves to be highlighted. I believe few coaches could have led the Eagles to be Super Bowl champions that season. Peterson was the right person for that particular time.

[39] Timothy J. Brown, "Public Memory as Contested Site: The Struggle for Existence at the National Museum of African American History and Culture," In *U.S. Public Memory, Rhetoric, and the National Mall*, ed. Roger Aden (Lanham: Lexington, 2018), 155-170.

[40] Quoted in James Dator, "LeBron James Opened a Public School in Akron for At-Risk Kids," *SBNATION*, July 30, 2018,

https://www.sbnation.com/nba/2018/7/30/17629560/lebron-james-i-promise-school-akron

Haiko's goal puts Whippets in finals

Downingtown needs OT to top Unionville

By TIM BROWN
RECORD Correspondent

Trick or treat came one day early for both Unionville High School and Downingtown High School's field hockey teams Wednesday.

After the Downingtown Whippets posted a grueling and emotional 1-0 overtime victory over Unionville at Conestoga to advance to Friday's PIAA District I Class AAA playoff final, there was no doubt who got the trick and who got the treat.

"It was deflected off of the defense," said a thrilled Deb DeLellis, coach of Downingtown. "(Jill) Haiko hit it and I don't know if it was going to go in, I don't know if it was a sure goal or whatever, but their defensive girl played it and it tapped off her stick and went in."

Jill Haiko's analysis went like this.

"Kristen Reily centered the ball across the circle and somehow I managed to slap it in," she said. "I was just aiming for the net, but it was going wide and one of their girls slapped it in."

The mystery goal which came with 3:05 left in the first overtime ended what had been a very competitive game between the the two local schools.

"It's a shame for the kids, because they played really hard," said a dejected Unionville coach, Sue Anderson, the former West Chester East standout.

From the outset, Unionville, which entered the game Southern Chester County League champions and unbeaten on the season, kept the pressure on the Downingtown defense and again the Whippets came up big.

Downingtown relied on numerous defensive plays like when sweeper Lori Donato stopped a two-on-one led by Unionville's Kathryn Smith.

And once again Kristen Gray gave her steady performance finishing with five saves in the Whippet cage.

"We were tentative in the midfield," said Haiko. "We were not really connecting and we didn't have many opportunities in the first half, but finally in the second half we were having our opportunities."

The Whippets did have their opportunities in the second half as they had all of their six penalty corners then.

"Second half they (Unionville) came out and were not rushing the ball as much, so we were able to build some momentum," said DeLellis.

Downingtown's best chance came midway through the second half off a corner.

Amy Whitesel took the corner pass and blasted it at the Unionville cage. There was a rebound off of Unionville goalie Erin Campbell, which caused a mad scramble in front of the net that left bodies on the ground.

The scoreless second half led to the decisive overtime.

Unionville had two more corners and two shots drilled by Kim Hicks,

(See HOCKEY, Page 11)

133

HOCKEY

(Continued from Page 10)

but once gain the Indians could not put the ball past Gray.

"We really thought we were going to pop one in," Anderson said. "Kim (Hicks) was hot on the corners in the overtime period, she really smoked two of them."

"They (Unionville) came out to play, they were fast, they were aggressive in the overtime, but we got the lucky break," said DeLellis.

The lucky break was a treat for the Whippets (14-5-2) as they will advance to the District I Class AAA title game Friday afternoon at Methacton High School against Central Bucks West, a 2-1 winner over West Chester East Wednesday.

Meanwhile Unionville (19-1-2) will have to deal with its first loss of the season and regroup for a District I state seeding game on Friday against East .

NOTES: Unionville outshot Downingtown 8-6 and had more penalty corners 14-6... Gray had 5 saves for the Whippets while Campbell had 3.

Appendix B: President Jimmy Carter Letter

To Tim Brown

I have read your research paper with care, and found it to be the best analysis of the 1980 Olympics issue that I have read. Although I do not agree with all of your points, such as the importance of federal funds for the USOC, the major thrust of your assertions are compatible with my own.

To answer your specific questions:

1. No. I really hoped that alternative games could be held if the Soviets did not withdraw from Afghanistan, and U.S. athletes could have an opportunity to demonstrate their prowess in international competition. As you know, the Olympics issue was just one of several that we pursued to guarantee that the Soviets would not be successful in taking Afghanistan and then moving into Pakistan and Iran. Two of the most important were the arming and support for Afghan freedom fighters and economic restraints.

2. No. As you have pointed out in your paper, the U.S. athletes were divided on the question, and as time passed seemed to be more against participation in Moscow. The overwhelming resolution in Congress accurately mirrored the attitude of American citizens. Only rarely on any controversial issue has public opinion been so clear and decisive. The U.S. ice hockey victory over the Soviet team at the Winter Olympics had a momentous impact. When I met at the White House with these Olympians, the mood was friendly and supportive.

3. I don't remember. You can examine the public record and see if this ever occurred.

4. My own preference would still be to have all the Summer Olympic games held in Greece, in an area that would be owned by the IOC. The excess commercialization is necessary in order to defray the enormous cost (more than $2 billion) of constructing a new site and hosting the events. The Winter games could be moved around. Every four years the choice of the host city is controversial, charged with politics, and divisive. Greece even boycotted Coca-Cola when Atlanta was chosen, and the Chinese people are now deeply resentful of the U.S. Congressional resolution against holding the 2000 games in Beijing. In general, though, I am sympathetic and supportive of the USOC and IOC and enjoy watching the ceremonies and contests on television.

Best wishes with your academic career, and thanks for taking an interest in one of the most difficult decisions I ever had to make. I will always believe that it was the correct one.

Jimmy Carter

1

135

About the Author

Timothy J. Brown, Ph.D. was born in Coatesville, Pennsylvania on July 12, 1969. He is the third of four children of Samuel H. Brown Jr. and Shirley M. Brown. As a youth, he enjoyed playing organized sports, neighborhood "pick-up" sports, board games with his siblings and the neighborhood kids, riding his bike, spending time with his immediate and extended family, and attending Coatesville Area Senior High School's Red Raider football and basketball games. As a high school student, he played football and basketball for the Red Raiders and graduated from Coatesville Area Senior High School in 1987.

After high school graduation, he attended West Chester University (WCU) where he earned his B.A. and M.A. degrees in Communication Studies. In between earning his bachelor's and master's degrees he was a sports reporter for the now defunct *Coatesville Record*. As a graduate student at WCU, he was awarded graduate assistantships with the Forensics (Speech and Debate) Team, the Frederick Douglass Institute, and as a teaching assistant to a large-lecture, mass communication course. Also, he was a tutor/course assistant for the Academic Development Program. After earning his M.A. from WCU, he enrolled at Ohio University as a doctoral student in the School of Interpersonal Communication's program (which is now the School of Communication Studies in the Scripps

College of Communication) where he was a graduate assistant for the Forensics Team. At Ohio University, he met Laura Hamilton Brown, Ph.D. who is now his wife. As an undergraduate student, he was employed during the summers at Pepperidge Farms in Downingtown, Pennsylvania, and as a graduate student he worked part-time in the house-keeping department at Chester County Hospital. Both experiences taught him lessons in working hard, being dependable, paying attention to detail, giving maximum effort and being a team player.

Currently, Dr. Brown serves as the Dean of Liberal Arts at Montogmery County Community College, Pennsylvania, where he oversees the following programs: Anthropology, Art, Communication Studies, Dance, English, ESL, History, Languages, Liberal Studies, Music, Philosophy, Political Science, Reading, Sociology, Strategies for College Success, and Theatre Arts. Prior to his current position, Dr. Brown was the Dean of the James L. Knight School of Communication at Queens University of Charlotte. Before Queens University, he was a Professor of Communication at West Chester University where he chaired the Department of Communication Studies for 10 years. At WCU he held numerous other leadership positions including Special Assistant to the Provost and Chair of the Council of Chairs. Prior to his time at WCU, he was a faculty member at Buffalo State College.

Dr. Brown is a rhetorical scholar whose research, teaching and consulting focus on the intersection of culture, communication, and identity. He has made over 80 presentations, most of which took place at the annual conferences of the National Communication Association (NCA) and the Eastern Communication Association (ECA). Examples of his publications include co-authoring the textbook *Public Speaking for Success: Strategies for Diverse Audiences and Occasions* (Hayden-McNeil). He was the second author of the textbook *Argumentation and Debate: A Public Speaking Approach* (Kendall/Hunt*)* and co-author of the article, "More Than a Game: Fulfilling Expectations and Inscriptions in the Career of LeBron James," published in *The Western Journal of Black Studies*. Also, he authored "Public Memory as Contested Site: The Struggle for Existence at the National Museum of African American History and Culture," published in the book, *U.S. Public Memory, Rhetoric, and the National Mall*.

On the national level, Dr. Brown has been a motivational speaker and workshop presenter on leadership skills for the Federal Government's Leadership Assessment Program. Moreover, Dr. Brown served on the National Communication Association's Learning Outcome's Project which created student learning outcomes for the Communication Studies discipline. For the Eastern Communication Association, he has served in a variety of capacities including Second Vice-President for its annual conference. In addition, he has been a workshop presenter on integrating diversity into the curriculum for the Educational Resources of New Jersey which provides professional development for public school teachers.

He has been honored by the Eastern Communication Association as a Distinguished Teaching Fellow and as a Distinguished Research Fellow. Also, he has received the association's Past President's Award. Furthermore, he was honored with the Drum Major for Justice Award by West Chester University's Frederick Douglass Society. Finally, he served on the Alumni Advisory Council for the School of Communication Studies at Ohio University.

His current hobbies include: playing and watching sports, coaching youth sports, reading, and writing. He and his wife, Laura Hamilton Brown, have two sons Jordan Josef Brown and Isaiah Hamilton Brown.

CPSIA information can be obtained
at www.ICGtesting.com
Printed in the USA
LVHW030153020721
691619LV00001B/23

9 780578 755519